EVIL INTRODUCTION

I must say, I'm surprised at you people. You actually fell for that whole "Austin Powers, sensitive writer" routine? Memo to publishing world: There's more talent on display in Mr. Bigglesworth's litter box than in any of Powers' work.

And then, on the other hand, there's me. I am an evil genius. Notice how, just before Austin's latest book – the one you are holding in your hands – was to be shipped, I instructed my precocious Lilliputian clone, Mini-Me, to intercept the printing process and had him insert my own "Evil Introduction." My capacity to be dastardly never ceases to amaze me, honestly. It's breathtaking.

And I have many other projects in the works, as well. The ink has yet to dry on a new TV deal I just signed. Sure, it's for basic cable, but I think that TBS is really the right vehicle for my *Dr. Evil's Def Bible Tales*. The networks, you see, just don't "get it."

Then construction is nearing completion for my franchised

theme restaurants, Evil Eye-Hop. The cuisine is nouvelle Cambodian: Be sure to try the Pol Pot Roast – it's heavenly.

And, of course, Mini-Me and I are developing a spoken word/performance art pas-de-deux to help promote the book on the talk-show circuit. It cleverly weaves the plot of a crewelwork needlepoint instructional video with an old concept album of mine concerning Namibian dairy products. We're still working out the kinks, but Letterman's people went wild for it.

By the way, should you be interested, I *am* available for public appearances – weddings, bar mitzvahs, that sort of thing. Call my agent.

Toodles,
Dr. Evil
Park City, Utah
February 1999

Shagadelically Speaking

Shagadelically Speaking

THE WORDS AND WORLD OF AUSTIN POWERS

LANCE GOULD

EBURY
PRESS

First published by Warner Books Inc; 1271 Avenue of the Americas, New York USA

3 5 7 9 10 8 6 4 2

Based on the screenplay by Mike Myers & Michael McCullers

First published in UK in 1999 by
Ebury Press
Random House, 20 Vauxhall Bridge Road, London SW1V 2SA

Random House Australia Pty Limited
20 Alfred Street, Milsons Point, Sydney, New South Wales 2061, Australia

Random House New Zealand Limited
18 Poland Road, Glenfield, Auckland 10, New Zealand

Random House South Africa (Pty) Limited
Endulini, 5A Jubilee Road, Parktown 2193, South Africa

Random House UK Limited Reg. No. 954009

A CIP catalogue record for this book is available from the British Library

ISBN 0 09 1871727

Book design and text composition by H. Roberts Design

Printed in Great Britain by Butler & Tanner Ltd.

Papers used by Ebury Press are natural, recyclable products made from wood grown in sustainable forests.

NEW LINE CINEMA Presents · AN ERIC'S BOY, MOVING PICTURES & TEAM TODD Production
A JAY ROACH Film · MIKE MYERS · AUSTIN POWERS: THE SPY WHO SHAGGED ME
HEATHER GRAHAM · MICHAEL YORK · ROBERT WAGNER · SETH GREEN · And ELIZABETH HURLEY
Music Supervisor JOHN HOULIHAN · Executive Music Producer DANNY BRAMSON · Music By GEORGE S. CLINTON
Costumes Designed By DEENA APPEL · Edited By JOHN POLL   DEBRA NEIL-FISHER
Production Designer RUSTY SMITH · Director of Photography UELI STEIGER
Executive Producers ERWIN STOFF   MICHAEL DE LUCA   DONNA LANGLEY
Produced By SUZANNE TODD   JENNIFER TODD   DEMI MOORE   ERIC McLEOD
Produced by JOHN LYONS MIKE MYERS
Written By MIKE MYERS & MICHAEL McCULLERS
Directed By Jay Roach
Based on Characters Created By Mike Meyers

Introduction

Salutations friends, fans, and
groovy birds. I'm so pleased you
decided to pick up my latest book,
*Shagadelically Speaking: The Words and
World of Austin Powers*. As many of you know, this is not the first
time I've put pen to paper. My earlier tomes include *Austin Powers'
Kama Sutra, Austin Powers' Sexy Dictionary, Swedish-Made
Penis-Enlarger Pumps and Me (This Sort of Thing Is My Bag, Baby)*,
and, of course, the white paper I composed on Caribbean macro-
economics in the NAFTA era, *Bahamian Rhapsody*.

And while I'm no Fyodor Dostoevsky or Jewel, I feel that I *have*
written enough to earn a place at the table of important contem-
porary authors. Or at least enough to challenge Norman Mailer to a
nude Jell-O–shot–drinking contest. Either way, there's no greater
feeling than knowing you've reached someone with your manuscript.
(My agent recently got word, in fact, that the Dewey Decimal System
people were going to specifically reserve ".69" for my work.)

That's where *Shagadelically Speaking* comes in. If it's happened
to me in my adventures, then it's in this book, luv. I've carefully

categorized all of my rites of passage and flights of fancy, in one comprehensive volume.

So fix yourself a martini, put a Burt Bacharach album on the turntable – hey, make that CD player! – and give this book a look-see. It's all here, baby, and it's all about me, yeah!

Clinky,

Austin Powers

London, England
February 1999

1/8 (one-eighth) Proportional size that Dr. Evil's clone, Mini-Me, represents of the original Dr. Evil.

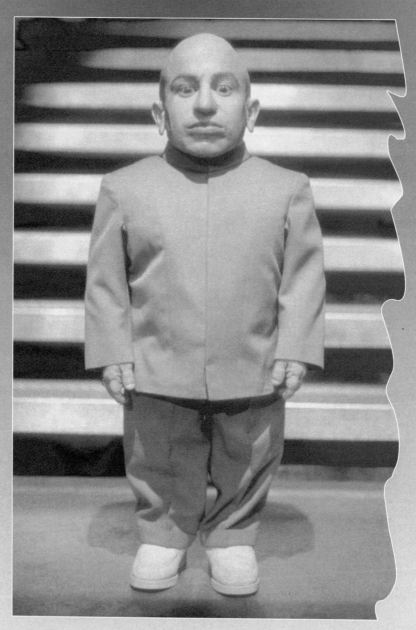

1 Number of inept guards who watch over the secret, doorless jail cell in Dr. Evil's volcano lair.

5 Total of the hand Austin is dealt when he plays the card game of blackjack, the object of which is to come as close to 21 without going over. It is hardly surprising that his hand of 5 does not win. "Cards are not my bag," Austin admits at the time.

6 Number of bullets an assassin fires at Austin in his old shag pad. Austin uses German spy Robin Swallows as a human shield. She takes the six bullets in the back.

9 millimeter automatic

Austin's gun and – as he was cryogenically frozen for thirty years and thus unaware of the dangers of unsafe sex – the only form of "protection" he uses when having intercourse with Alotta Fagina.

11 Number of synchronized swimmers Austin leads in an elaborate routine in the pool of his honeymoon hotel in France.

19 Scott Evil's age in 1999.

25 Number of hours Austin's marriage to Vanessa lasts.

27 Number of countries that allegedly broadcast *The Jerry Springer Show,* to an alleged 50 million viewers. At least that's what Springer tells his guest, Dr. Evil.

50 kilowatt The power of the nuclear warhead that Dr. Evil has hijacked from Kreplachistan and attached to his earth-drilling Vulcan, with which he plans to destroy the world.

69 A number very close to Austin's heart. When Basil warns him to be wary of the differences in culture between 1999 and 1969, Austin says, "Don't worry, Basil, sixty-nine's my favorite number. Ow! Yeah!"

1967 The year in which Austin was first cryogenically frozen. He was later reanimated in 1997.

1969 The year to which Dr. Evil travels in time from 1999.

$100 billion Ransom payment Dr. Evil demands from the United Nations in 1997 to prevent him from executing Project Vulcan. (He later reveals, however, that he will execute his dastardly plan whether the UN pays him or not.) He initially seeks only $1 million, until his second-in-command, Number 2, advises him that a million bucks is not as impressive a booty in 1997 as it may have been in 1967.

$1 kajillion bajillion Figure the president of the United States mockingly suggests Dr. Evil might as well ask for when the latter demands a $100 billion payment in order to save Washington, D.C., from being destroyed by his Alan Parsons Project. The president and his advisors laugh, doubting that "a hundred billion is even a number."

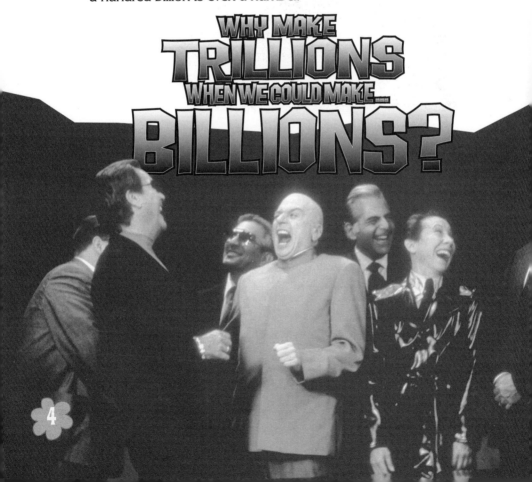

a-hole More polite form of "asshole," though still vulgar. What Dr. Evil calls Austin after the latter shoots him in the leg.

American Dialect of English spoken in the colonies, and the only language in which Felicity is fluent. When Austin tries to convey to her in his inimitable English that he is temporarily impotent, he instead merely confuses her, prompting her to demand that he "Speak American."

America Online Internet service provider renowned for its "You've got mail!" salutation. Basil uses America Online to videoconference Austin on a laptop computer. In 1999, an Austinified salutation is updated to say, "You've got mail, baby!"

anal-retentive behavior Condition suffered by Vanessa, most clearly manifest in her habit of stuffing all the items in her suitcase into little individual plastic baggies and labeling them.

Apollo 11 The U.S. space program's manned mission to the moon. Seems that its 1969 blastoff is actually delayed so that Austin and Felicity can come aboard, incognitolike. They take the flight in order to tangle with Dr. Evil on the moon.

ass Insulting term often utilized by Scott Evil to ridicule his father, as when he mockingly informs his unaware dad that "It's 1969 – Jerry Maguire won't come out for another thirty years, ass."

THE SWINGER HAS LANDED

Austin's father After Austin shoots Dr. Evil in the leg, it looks as if Austin is going to finish him off. That's when Dr. Evil proffers a stunning confession: "Austin, I am . . . your . . . father." Flabbergasted, Austin replies, "Really?" To which Dr. Evil says, "No. I can't back that up. I was just grasping at straws. I had nothing."

I MAKE THE DECISIONS HERE. I DEMAND A LITTLE RESPECT.

Bacharach, Burt Treacly 1960s singer/songwriter and favorite of aging hipsters. He performs a nighttime serenade for Austin and Vanessa atop a double-decker tourist bus in Las Vegas with his classic love tune "What the World Needs Now." Earlier, when Austin collects his valuables after having been cryogenically frozen, he finds among them a vinyl Burt Bacharach album, *Burt Bacharach Plays His Hits.* Yet another Bacharach album is among Austin's few remaining possessions in his old shag pad, along with a lava lamp. Bacharach and Elvis Costello later serenade Felicity and Austin.

Back to the future Successful though tiresome series of 1980s time-travel films starring Michael J. Fox. When his own time travel leaves Austin thoroughly confused about who and where he is, he admits, "It makes you wonder how Michael J. Fox did all those *Back to the Future* movies."

bag Something of interest to an individual. Austin denotes his lack of interest in blackjack by saying, "Cards are not my bag, baby."

bag, burlap As a child, when Dr. Evil was insolent, he was placed in a burlap bag and beaten with reeds.

bag of sshhh! Metaphorical entity held in reserve by Dr. Evil for his too-loquacious son, Scott. See **Sshhh!**

baggie See **salad tongs**.

bagpipes Musical instrument, the evocation of which is a frequent – though hackneyed – method of conveying something Scottish. When Scotsman Fat Bastard steals Austin's mojo, he pulls out a set of bagpipes that emits a white vaporous nerve gas, knocking out the armed soldiers guarding Austin's cryogenically frozen body.

baldness Condition of hairlessness suffered by both Dr. Evil and his pet domestic cat, Mr. Bigglesworth. Ironically, the hairless Evil resides at the opposite end of the follicle spectrum from his quite hirsute archnemesis, Austin Powers.

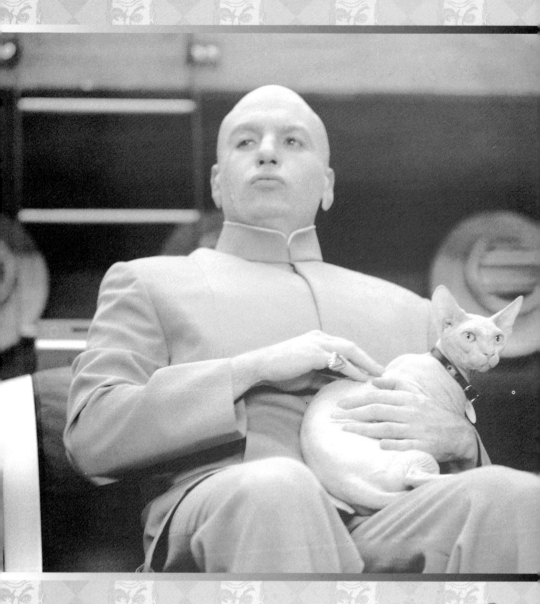

ball bearings Material used in the manufacturing of a Fembot. Austin discovers too late that Vanessa is "constructed of plastic, wires, ball bearings, what-have-you."

Band-Aid Sticky gauze bandage used to cover up minor cuts and abrasions, enabling them to heal more readily. Also employed later by Number 2 to help heal the bite wounds left on his fingers by the vicious Mini-Me after the two simulltaneously reach for the same cookies.

baseball An American pastime. Austin concentrates on this unsexy activity to avoid succumbing to the deadly sexual advances of the Fembots.

Bastard, Fat Dr. Evil's spy within the Ministry of Defense (M.O.D.). A scotsman, Bastard also seems to be loosely connected to a Scottish independence movement. He steals Austin's mojo for Dr. Evil. He is also monstrously obese. He acquired the nickname Fat Bastard because he is "the incorrect weight for my height, and I was born out of wedlock."

bazooka See **human shield**.

I'VE GOT A LOT OF DEMONS KICKIN' AROUND IN MY NOGGIN, BUT WEIGHT ISSUES AIN'T ONE OF THEM.

beard, fake Hairpiece that covers the jowls, chin, and cheeks. Often employed to conceal one's identity while one is eluding pursuers. Austin uses a fake beard to escape his adoring British groupies in 1967.

Beavis and Butt-head Parentally maligned MTV cartoon characters occasionally cited for teaching children the wonderful ways of arson. As Dr. Evil attempts to sign off his dastardly broadcast to the United Nations – during which he reveals his intention to destroy the world—he mistakenly switches their television monitors to a broadcast of a *Beavis and Butt-head* episode.

Beefeater See **United Nations' Secret Meeting Room.**

bell Device that makes ringing noise. When Dr. Evil can't find his trusty sidekick Mini-Me (unbeknownst to Dr. Evil, Mini-Me's chair has gone haywire, sending him up toward the ceiling), he becomes agitated. "Mini-Me? Hello?" he shouts. "Can we put a frickin' bell on him or something?"

Berlin Wall Heavily guarded wall/fence separating West Berlin from the rest of the city, erected by the East German government in 1961 to prevent its citizens from

escaping into the freer West. The fall of the Wall in 1989 signaled the end of Communism in Eastern Europe; Austin, however, only learns of this event eight years later while watching a videotape of historic events that he missed while he was cryogenically frozen.

Bigglesworth, Mr. Dr. Evil's pussy, who loses all his hair in the cryogenic process. Like Dr. Evil, Mr. Bigglesworth has a clone that is identical to him in every way except for the fact that the clone is only one-eighth the size of

bin, overhead storage Compartment on a commercial airplane intended to store carry-on bags and small items. One reason Dr. Evil can emotionally afford to have lost all interest in his son, Scott, is because of his special relationship with his small clone, Mini-Me. Dr. Evil taunts Scott by noting that Mini-Me "is evil, he wants to take over the world, and he fits easily into most overhead storage bins."

bird American astronaut slang, apparently, for "space shuttle." So it seems, anyway, after Condor, an astronaut in orbit, tells his Houston, Texas, headquarters that he is "outside the bird." Also, British slang for "babe" or "chick."

bird, groovy What Austin adoringly calls Felicity.

bitch, sexy Austin's self-image. "I'm striking," 1999 Austin says with confidence while looking at his 1967 cryo genically frozen self. "I'm downright handsome. I'm a sexy bitch."

bitchslapping Misogynistic term for physical abuse popularized in gangsta rap music and seen frequently on daytime TV talk-show melees. Dr. Evil bitchslaps a Klansman during a taping of *The Jerry Springer Show*.

bits and pieces One of the many nicknames Austin has conferred on his genitalia.

block and tackle See **pulleys, elaborate set of.**

"Blow me" The retort of Dr. Evil's son, Scott, upon being asked by his father whether or not he wants "to see what Daddy does for a living."

Bob's Big Boy American fast-food restaurant chain whose mascot is a cherubic (some might say fat) little boy maniacally holding a plate of burgers and whatnot. Dr. Evil's spaceship is a flying replica of a Bob's Big Boy mascot.

bodies bursting into flames The inept guard watching over Austin and Felicity in Dr. Evil's secret hollowed-out volcano-lair jail cell bursts into the cell to take a gander at Felicity's exposed jubblies. He then falls into a pit of bubbling, liquid-hot magma below and bursts into flames.

Bolton Creepy redheaded tour guide of the Virtucon facility. He uses a walkie-talkie to inform his superiors that Austin and Vanessa have improperly entered a restricted area on Dr. Evil's property.

book, Swedish-Made Penis-Enlarger Pumps and Me (This Sort of Thing Is My Bag, Baby), by Austin Powers One of the items kept in storage for Austin while he is cryogenically frozen.

boots, Italian, one pair One of the items kept in storage for Austin while he is cryogenically frozen. When they are returned to him, he greets them in their native tongue: "Buongiorno, boys."

boulangerie A French bakery. Dr. Evil's father owned a boulangerie in his native Belgium.

bra-burning 1960s and 1970s feminist political statement, metaphorically freeing women – and their breasts – from the shackles of the male-dominated

establishment. Felicity, who tells Austin that she's a feminist, invites him to a feminist "rally." At first he notes that he's not exactly the political type, but when he finds out that all of the participants are "going to take [their] bras and burn them," he asks enthusiastically, "What time does it start?"

buggery Sodomy. Dr. Evil's father, it is learned in a group therapy session, had a penchant for it.

burned, very badly In 1997, Mustafa is "very badly burned" when Dr. Evil presses the MUSTAFA button on his deadly control panel, sending him into the fiery pit. In 1969, Mustafa is "very badly burned" yet again when he falls off a cliff, tumbles down a mountain, and explodes.

bus, double-decker tourist Two-tiered sightseeing vehicle, usually painted red, the evocation of which is a frequent – though clichéd – method of conveying something British, particularly London. Burt Bacharach performs a nighttime serenade for Austin and Vanessa atop one in Las Vegas with his classic love tune "What the World Needs Now." The bus is owned by Her Majesty's Vegas Tours.

business card Small card providing crucial information about an individual. Austin demonstrates poor judgment when he brings his silver business-card carrying case with him to the penthouse apartment of Alotta Fagina while he is supposed to be undercover as Richie Cunningham. Fagina discovers his silver case and spies his business card, which reads AUSTIN POWERS, INTERNATIONAL MAN OF MYSTERY, and is adorned with the male symbol.

button, Abort Last-resort, emergency-stop mechanism in Project Vulcan. Austin is able to hit the button just as the world's time is about to expire, thus aborting Project Vulcan and preventing the detonation of a Kreplachistani warhead in the earth's core.

button, Self-Destruct Button that, when pressed, implodes Dr. Evil's moon base. Dr. Evil presses it when he realizes Austin has foiled him yet again, then escapes into his time portal.

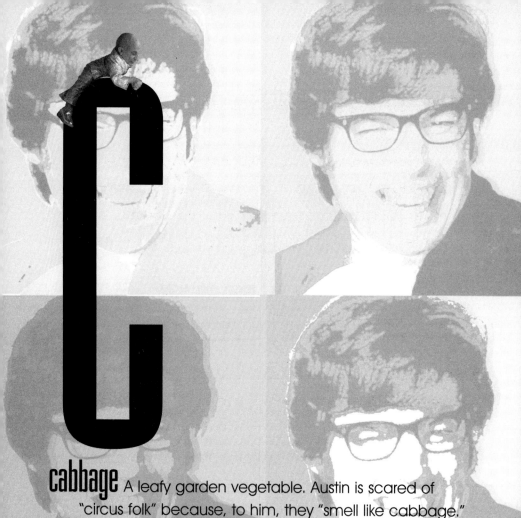

cabbage

A leafy garden vegetable. Austin is scared of "circus folk" because, to him, they "smell like cabbage."

cable television

Virtucon owns cable television companies in thirty-eight states. While snooping around in Alotta Fagina's penthouse, Austin discovers that the entire cable enterprise is a cover-up operation, at least according to Virtucon's business-plan pyramid. Virtucon's real interest lies in destroying the world, trafficking in human organs, and producing a Carrot Top movie.

carnal ecstasy, night of How Fat Bastard characterizes his shag session with Felicity.

LOOK AT ME, I'M A BIG FAT SLOB.

Carrot Top Movie
One of Virtucon's three secret diabolical projects. The others are Human Organ Trafficking and Project Vulcan.

Cass, Mama
See **"People I Know" list; ham sandwich.**

ceiling
Where Mini-Me ends up when his electronic chair goes haywire. "My frickin' mascot is stuck to the ceiling, okay?" complains Dr. Evil to his staff. "Not good. Papa not happy."

Celebrity Vault
Subsection of the Ministry of Defense's Cryogenic Storage Center where celebrities such as Gary Coleman and Vanilla Ice are stored for safe-keeping in a cryogenically frozen state.

champagne Fine, often French, sparkling wine. At one point on their honeymoon, Vanessa squeezes a champagne bottle until it breaks, causing Austin some consternation. It is soon after revealed that Vanessa is a Fembot.

Chapter Eleven Chapter in Austin's book *Austin Powers' Kama Sutra* that Austin and Vanessa have reached on their sexually active honeymoon. Subsequent chapters describe such sexual positions as The Wheelbarrow, The Praying Donkey, and The Chinese Shag Swing.

cheating When one person in a committed relationship has sexual relations outside that relationship without permission. When one person in a committed relationship has sex with another "version" of the other person in the relationship, however, all bets are off. "Technically, it ain't cheating," says Past Austin, in bed with Felicity, as a stunned Regular Austin looks on.

chess Game of strategy in which two opponents each control the movements of a warring kingdom. Ivana Humpalot notes that it takes a keen intelligence to play chess, and that men with big brains make better lovers. Demonstrating his breadth of knowledge of the game, Austin notes that "The horsie . . . moves in an L shape."

chestnuts Edible nuts of a chestnut tree. Dr. Evil's father often accused them of being lazy.

chicken Food product that Fat Bastard offers Felicity in bed after they finish making love.

Chinese Shag Swing, The *See* **Powers' Kama Sutra, Austin.**

Christ, Jesus According to the Christian faith, the son of God. Also, an expression of disbelief, as in when Fat Bastard lays eyes on Mini-Me for the first time: "Jesus Christ, he's tiny. I've had bigger chunks of corn in my crap."

CIA Central Intelligence Agency of the United States, an outfit to which Felicity belongs. Spies, baby, and they're Yanks.

clap, the Nickname for gonorrhea, a venereal disease. Austin lets it slip that he picked up a case of the clap in November 1964, in the Dutch East Indies, while on shore leave. Penicillin, the miracle drug, he adds, took care of it. He accidentally reveals this information after Ivana Humpalot asks him when he got the Clapper, a cheesy electronic device. *See* **Clapper, the.**

Clapper, the Device, primarily for the elderly and the aesthetically impaired, that can turn an appliance on or off with a clap of the hands. It does not seem to be sold in stores, but is usually made available for limited periods of time in exclusive television offers. Austin has one in his new shag pad.

cleansing *See* **Reanimation Process.**

cleavage, butt Space between two butt cheeks. It is in Fat Bastard's butt cleavage that Felicity places a homing devise, after shagging him.

clichés, movie When they are pursued in a high-speed car chase by one of Dr. Evil's henchmen. Felicity says to Austin, "We've got company,"

"Clinky" Uniquely Austin-esque toast, like "Cheers," proffered when he and Alotta Fagina raise their champagne glasses in her hot tub. *See* **L'chaim.**

cloning Replication of an organic entity through the use of a complicated cell-duplication process. In 1997, after Dr. Evil rockets into space in a frozen cryogenic state for the second time, his associates initiate a program to clone him. Dr. Evil's clone, Mini-Me, is identical to him in every way, except that he is one-eighth Dr. Evil's size. Mr. Bigglesworth, Dr. Evil's pet pussy, is also cloned in smaller form.

coffee imaginable—ever, cup of the most foul-smelling

While waiting for the results of Fat Bastard's stool sample to come in, Austin intends to pour himself a cup of Joe, but instead accidentally pours himself a cup of "Nooooo!"

cold shower

Austin contemplates this most unsexual activity to avoid succumbing to the deadly sexual advances of the Fembots.

Cold War

Lengthy political war of ideology and tension manifested in an enduring animosity between Western and Eastern powers. This war is generally recognized as having been "won" by Western ideology in the late 1980s and early 1990s. The outcome of said battle, however, remains unknown to Austin in his cryogenically frozen state. *See* **pigs, capitalist.**

Coleman, Gary

See **Celebrity Vault.**

Comrade

See **pigs, capitalist.**

condom

Prophylactic device used to prevent pregnancies and the transmission of venereal diseases. In Austin's mind, however, they are used only by sailors.

Condor

Code name of the American astronaut outside his space shuttle who has a close encounter in space with Dr. Evil's Bob's Big Boy rocket.

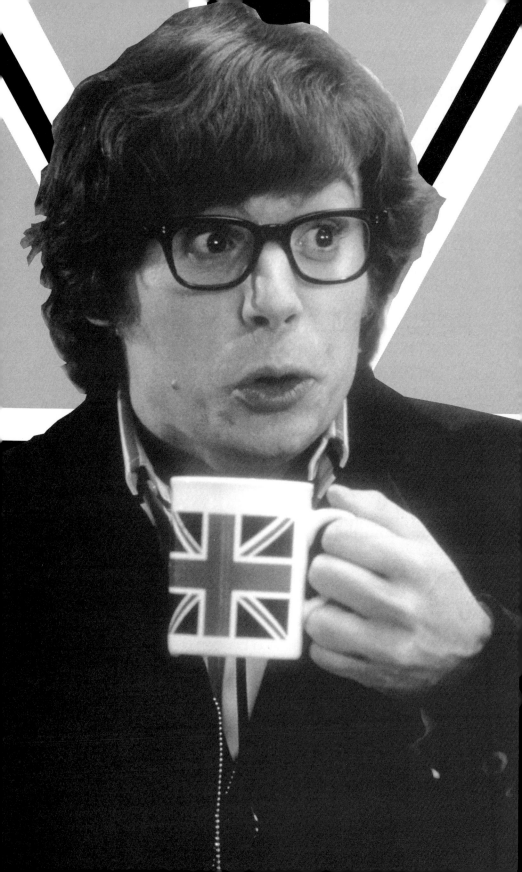

control panel

Though it looks like a phone programmed with various names in speed-dial, Dr. Evil can use his control panel to bring instant death to any of his various associates by tipping them upside down out of their boardroom chairs into a fiery pit. Occasionally, however, it malfunctions, as when Dr. Evil presses the MUSTAFA button and Mustafa is simply "very badly burned." Ironically, Mustafa designed the control panel and the fiery pit, shortly before being tossed into it.

cookies, plate of

Treats Dr. Evil serves his associates. Mini-Me so enjoys the tasty cookies, in fact, that he lunges at others who attempt to take cookies off of the plate, as evidenced by all of the Band-Aids on Number 2's fingers.

corn, chunks of

Fat Bastard divulges that some of the "chunks of corn" in his "crap" are bigger than the tiny Mini-Me.

corpse, headless

After Austin and Vanessa shove the head of one of Dr. Evil's henchmen into a tank filled with ill-tempered, mutated sea bass, the henchman's head is bitten off entirely. Later, when Austin lands two wild judo chops simultaneously to the henchman's head – causing it to explode like a balloon filled with foie gras in a microwave – all that is left of the henchman is a headless corpse.

Costello, Elvis

New Wave pop singer. He serenades Felicity and Austin with Burt Bacharach.

courtesy flush

Crude but often appreciated gesture from one person in a rest-room stall to another rest-room patron, usually in an adjoining stall, to help eradicate invasive foul odors. A gregarious Texan stranger asks Austin for a courtesy flush after hearing what he presumed to be Austin's struggle with an altogether different type of Number 2.

crap on deck

Bowel movement that is quite ready to come out on its own accord. When Fat Bastard reveals that he needs to find a bathroom right away, he semaphores the urgency of his request by noting that he's "got a crap on deck that could choke a donkey."

crapper

Toilet. When people are on the crapper, they are vulnerable. That is why Scott Evil suggests to his father that Dr. Evil simply go back in time "and kill Austin Powers when he's on the crapper or something." To which his father replies, "No, no, Scott. The truly evil murder with style."

cravat, frilly lace One of the items kept in storage for Austin while he is cryogenically frozen.

credit card receipt for Swedish-made penis-enlarger pump, signed by Austin Powers One of the items kept in storage for Austin while he is cryogenically frozen.

cricket Accepted, polite behavior. When Felicity kicks Fat Bastard in the testicles, Austin chides her, "I don't care if he is a bastard, you don't kick a man in the pills. It just ain't cricket, baby."

crikey Mild British euphemism for "Christ." When Austin realizes all is not well with his meat and two bits, he has an epiphany: "Crikey, I've lost my mojo."

cross-mojination Struggle between two equally compelling mojo forces. When two mojos are simultaneously working against one another, the result can be deadly. Austin prevails in his battle with the Fembots solely because his mojo is superior. *See* **mojo.**

cryogenics Science of freezing an individual for future use as one would a steak, a waffle, or a human organ.

Cryogenic Storage Center Room in the London head-quarters of the Ministry of Defense (M.O.D.) where Austin is stored for thirty years in a cryogenically frozen state.

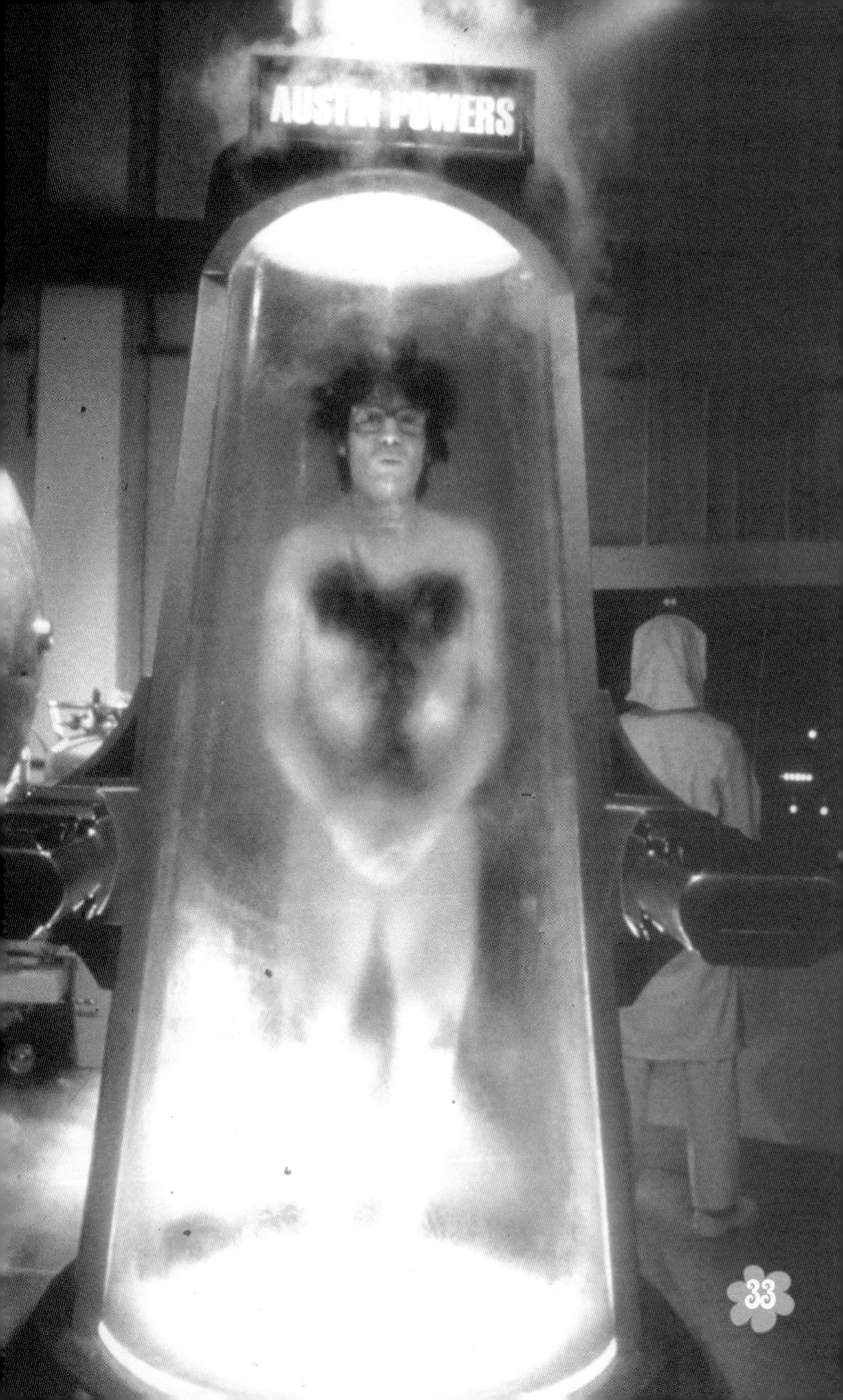
AUSTIN POWERS

Cunningham, Oprah Alias Vanessa uses when she and Austin meet Dr. Evil's second-in-command, Number 2, and his "Italian confidential secretary, " Alotta Fagina.

Cunningham, Richie Alias Austin uses when he and Vanessa meet Dr. Evil's second-in-command, Number 2, and his "Italian confidential secretary," Alotta Fagina.

cycloptic Having one eye; a politically incorrect adjective uttered by Dr. Evil in reference to his eye-patch–wearing second-in-command, Number 2, as when he refers to Number 2 as his "cycloptic colleague."

Danger Austin's middle name. Really. As in Austin Danger Powers.

death, overly elaborate and exotic When
Dr. Evil has Austin in his clutches, he introduces him to his son, Scott. Scott is surprised and annoyed that his father doesn't simply shoot his archnemesis, but Dr. Evil has grander plans for Austin: "I'm going to put him in an easily escapable situation involving an overly elaborate and exotic death."

Death Star Dr. Evil wants to "turn the moon into what I like to call a Death Star," by installing a powerful laser with which he can destroy any of the earth's cities. When Scott snickers upon hearing this plan, his father demands to know what is so funny. "Nothing, Darth," says his insolent son.

dental hygiene, poor Condition in which one's teeth are not well cared for, manifestations of which are bad breath, misshapen molars, and generally unpleasant if not earnest smiles. Like most Brits, Austin does not practice the highest grade of dental hygiene. Vanessa's mother, Mrs. Kensington, notes, however, that, in Britain in the 1960s, "bad teeth did not necessarily affect your sex-symbol status." Ironically, both toothpaste and dental floss play key roles in Austin and Vanessa's escape from the clutches of Dr. Evil's "overly elaborate" plan to liquidate them. Later, when Austin travels back in time, his teeth revert to their former horrid state.

dipping mechanism, unnecessarily slow-moving Device used by Dr. Evil when he attempts to liquidate Austin and Vanessa. Placed on the unnecessarily slow-moving dipping mechanism, Austin and Vanessa are to be slowly dipped into a tank of ill-tempered, mutated sea bass. Thanks to an array of dental products, however, they are able to escape.

dirty pillows Female breasts. When Austin gets his face wedged into Felicity's cleavage, he notes that "I seem to be stuck in your dirty pillows."

YEAH, BABY, GRRR!

disposal Room in Dr. Evil's moon base from which Mini-Me is flushed into outer space, through the garbage disposal.

"Doctaaaarrrrrri!" Frightening war whoop yelled by Mustafa when he charges at Austin with a big curved knife. The precise meaning of "Doctaaaarrrrrri!" is unclear.

Donkey, The Praying *See* **Powers' Kama Sutra, Austin.**

Don Luigi
One of Dr. Evil's henchmen. Don Luigi is, presumably, a gangster. At Dr. Evil's initial Virtucon board-room meeting, we see Don Luigi, who has only one human hand, smoking a cigar he holds with his claw hand. When Dr. Evil presses the DON LUIGI button on his deadly control panel, the Don tumbles backward into the fiery pit. The next time we see Dr. Evil's control panel, Don Luigi's name is no longer listed.

donnybrook
Melee; a free-for-all; a brawl. A fight between Dr. Evil and a Klansman develops into a donnybrook during a taping of *The Jerry Springer Show.*

"Don't go there, girlfriend"
Expression popularized in the 1990s on daytime talk shows such as *The Rikki Lake Show* and *The Oprah Winfrey Show.* When the president of the United States calls Dr. Evil a "nutbar," Dr. Evil warns him, "Don't go there, girlfriend."

dope
What Scott Evil calls his father, mocking him. Mini-Me is so enraged by this audacious act of insolence that he attempts to press the SCOTT EVIL button on Dr. Evil's deadly control panel. Mini-Me is stopped at the last moment by Frau Farbissina, who sprays the little cretin with a water bottle.

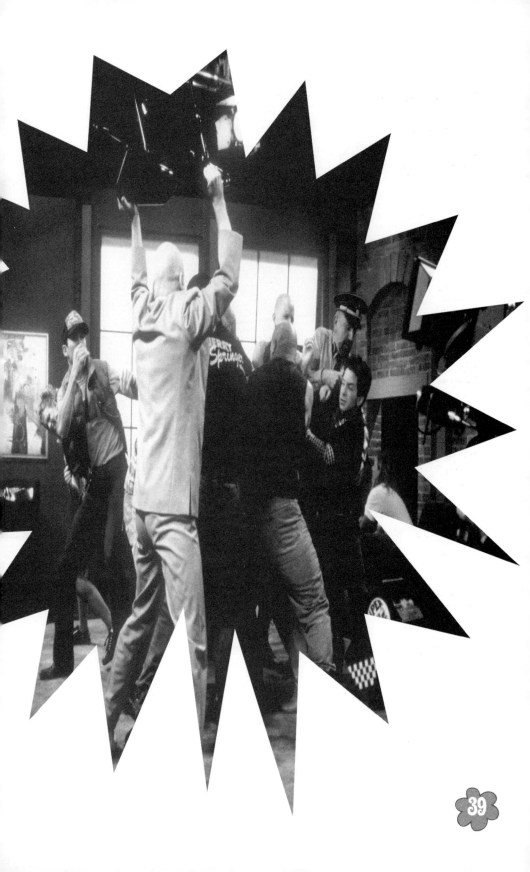

39

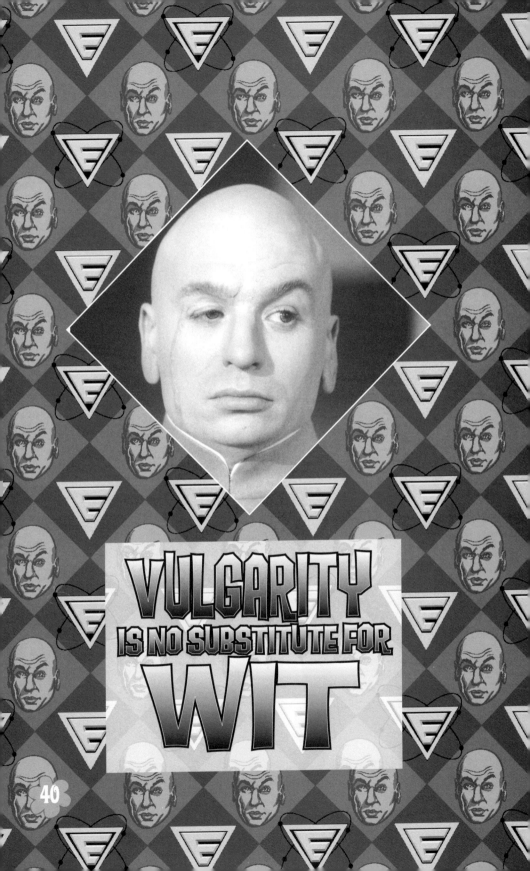

VULGARITY IS NO SUBSTITUTE FOR WIT

40

"Eibe wein in scheinin" German for "Let's get it on"; what Frau Farbissina urges Dr. Evil to do when she succumbs to his mojo-nacious ways in their "private-time" session.

Einstein One of the most brilliant men to ever live. The name can also be utilized as a sarcastic insult, such as when Scott Evil lets his father know what he thinks about sending Austin and Felicity to his volcano-lair jail cell. "Good plan, Einstein," he says, mockingly. "The jail cell doesn't even have a door."

Electric Psychedelic Pussycat Swinger's Club

Popular nightspot in 1960s London, frequented by Austin and Mrs. Kensington. It is also the scene where a party in Austin's honor is held, during which a botched assassination attempt on his life occurs. This club is also the spot where Austin and Dr. Evil have their last face-to-face battle in 1967, and the spot from atop which Dr. Evil gets away in his Bob's Big Boy rocket, cryogenically freezing himself and his cat, Mr. Bigglesworth, as he blasts into space.

Elite Moon Unit
Force comprising all the personnel on Dr. Evil's moon base. The Elite Moon Unit is broken down into two groups, Moon Unit Alpha and Moon Unit Zappa.

endangered species
Any of various species of fauna or flora that are considered endangered due to their dwindling numbers. Dr. Evil used to use sharks to dispose of unwanted visitors, but, as Number 2 informs him, because sharks are now considered an endangered species, they have had to substitute sea bass. More specifically, ill-tempered, mutated sea bass.

evacuation
See **Reanimation Process.**

43

Evil, Dr. Head of a worldwide evil organization that has aspirations for world domination. Archnemesis of Austin Powers. Completely bald, he sports a face-length scar on his right cheek. Sartorially, he favors a 1960s tyrannical despot look and can often be found in a Nehru jacket.

evil empire Well-organized, mean-spirited, amoral operation, mandate of which is usually world domination. When Scott Evil ridicules the names Dr. Evil has chosen for his evil operations (e.g., Death Star, Alan Parsons Project), Dr. Evil points to his laser and says, "When you get your own evil empire, you can call it whatever you want."

Evil Medical School Institution from which Dr. Evil earned his medical degree.

Evil, Scott Dr. Evil's son. At first Dr. Evil and Scott are both led to believe that while Dr. Evil was cryogenically frozen, his frozen sperm was tapped to produce an heir, and thus was Scott born.

Exposition, Basil Austin's immediate superior in British Intelligence.

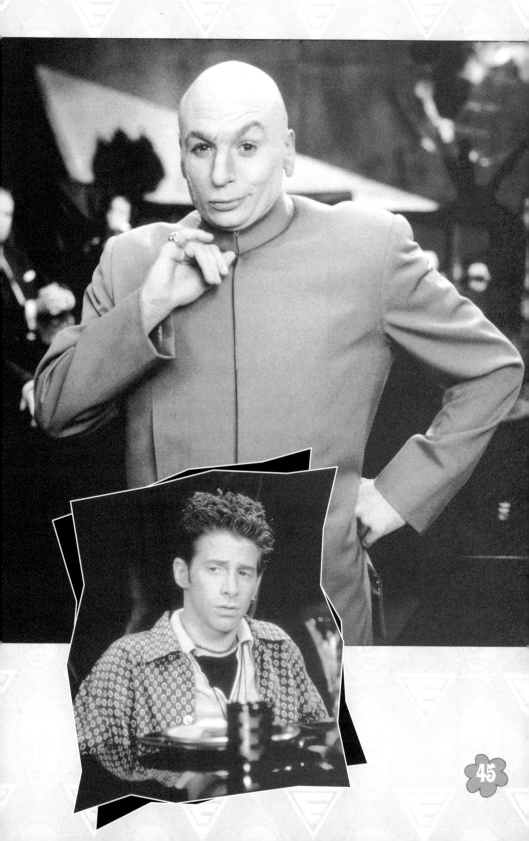

Exposition, Mrs. Mother of Basil. Austin mistakes her for a man and knocks her out with a vicious right uppercut. Austin explains to a flabbergasted Basil that his mother is rather "mannish" and "looks like she was beaten with an ugly stick."

eye-patch X-ray vision *See* X-ray vision, eye-patch.

Fab! magazine
British celebrity magazine of the 1960s. Austin hides behind a copy of *Fab!* to escape his adoring British groupies in 1967. His face also happens to grace the cover of that particular issue.

factory that makes miniature models of factories
Virtucon owns one in Chicago, Illinois.

Fagina, Alotta

Number 2's "Italian confidential secretary." Austin breaks into the apartment of this melon-breasted femme fatale in an attempt to secure more information about Project Vulcan. He ends up having a romantic encounter with Fagina ("I shagged her rotten!" he brags to Vanessa).

familial relations, strained

Scott Evil and his pop, Dr. Evil, don't exactly see eye-to-lazy-eye. Dr. Evil was never there for Scott growing up (he was in space, actually, in a cryogenically frozen state – the two did not meet until Scott was seventeen). They try group therapy; Scott admits to a fondness for animals and Dr. Evil recalls having worn meat helmets in the springs of his youth. But Dr. Evil soon has the group liquidated because they are insolent.

Farbissina, Frau

One of Dr. Evil's
henchwomen. She
leads a fractious
militant wing of the
Salvation Army.
A matronly figure,
she uses a small
whip to prevent
Dr. Evil from press-
ing a button on his
control panel that
would liquidate his
son, Scott.

fart Expulsion of intestinal gas, often considered vulgar. Austin lets loose in the hot tub of melon-breasted femme fatale Alotta Fagina, which prompts him to write an apologetic poem.

fashion photography The profession that Austin uses as his nonspying "cover."

Fembots "The latest word in android replicant technology," these sirenous maneaters equipped with nipple guns and dressed like vixens are robots designed for the express purpose of charming and disarming men . . . and then killing them.

fiery pit Dr. Evil's flaming hole of murder and despair, designed by Mustafa. If Dr. Evil is unhappy with an underling's work, a button on his deadly control panel allows him to send the henchman's chair tumbling backward into the fiery pit.

finger, the Insulting gesture in which an individual extends the middle digit on his or her hand and directs it toward another individual. After Mini-Me tries unsuccessfully to kill Scott Evil by reaching for the Scott Evil button on Dr. Evil's deadly control panel – he is stopped by Frau Farbissina when she squirts him with a water bottle – Mini-Me glares at Scott and instead gives him the finger.

Flock of Seagulls, A A 1980s New Wave band more noteworthy for its silly extended-bang hairdos than for its musical legacy. When Felicity expresses a desire to see the 1970s and 1980s – as opposed to jumping directly into the 1990s through time travel – Austin assures her that she is not missing anything. "I looked into it," he says. "There's a gas shortage and A Flock of Seagulls. That's about it."

food poisoning Austin volunteers "to pretend to be desperately ill with food poisoning" to help himself and Felicity escape from Dr. Evil's secret hollowed-out volcano-lair jail cell. Felicity's plan, to flash her jubblies at the guard, proves more effective.

footage Excerpt from a film or videotape. When Dr. Evil shows the president of the United States a video of the White House being blown up as an ominous warning; the president thinks this is actually taking place. Dr. Evil then patiently explains that the video was actually footage from the film *Independence Day*.

Forbes magazine Leading American business publication founded by millionaire Malcolm Forbes, late father of perennial losing American presidential candidate Steve Forbes. Dr. Evil's second-in-command, Number 2, laments the fact that, were it not for Dr. Evil's meddling and his greedy desire to take over the world, Virtucon would have continued to perform steadily, allowing Number 2 to have been the subject of a cover story in *Forbes*.

foreign languages Vanessa's course of study at world-renowned Oxford University.

52

foreplay Preamble to the sex act, usually performed to prepare both participants for said act. Despite his vaunted reputation as a love-maker, Austin lacks in this area. The best evidence we have of this comes from the Fembot Vanessa, who, it turns out, has machine-gun jubblies. Austin fails to notice them during their love-making, a fact Vanessa attributes to Austin's inadequacies in the foreplay department.

Freud, Dr. World's most renowned psychiatrist, Sigmund Freud. When Regular Austin admits that seeing Past Austin in bed with Felicity makes him "very randy," Past Austin yells, "Paging Dr. Freud!"

frozen semen After Dr. Evil has been in space in a frozen cryogenic state for a number of years, his associates get worried and, using Evil's frozen sperm, produce an Evil heir to carry on the Evil name. Dr. Evil's son, Scott, is thus born. Later, it is revealed that this entire story was actually created to protect the identity of Scott's mother, Frau Farbissina.

fruit basket Basil gives a fruit basket to Austin and Vanessa as a wedding present.

F-sharp Musical key in which Dr. Evil is playing the Joan Osborne classic ditty "What If God Was One of Us?" in a piano duet with Mini-Me, who plays along in the wrong key.

future, ominous vision of the Austin is not beyond making Felicity the victim of his naughty pranks. One such devilish stunt sees Austin telling Felicity what she can expect in the 1990s: "flying cars," "entire meals in pill form," and an "earth ruled by damn dirty apes." Before she can get her knickers in a twist, however, he lets her in on his little joke.

Future Austin One of many Austins. This particular Austin is the one who saves Felicity while Past Austin "saves the world." He is also known as Austin From Ten Minutes From Now.

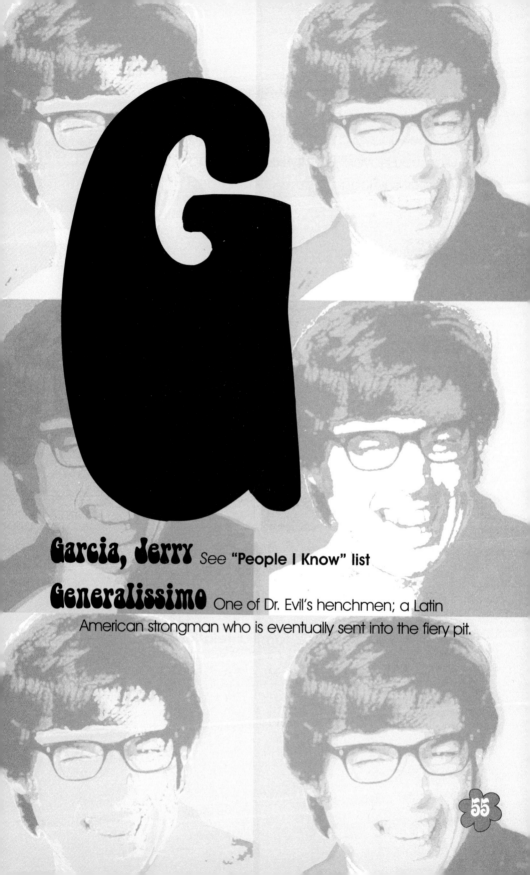

G

Garcia, Jerry *See "People I Know" list*

Generalissimo One of Dr. Evil's henchmen; a Latin American strongman who is eventually sent into the fiery pit.

girth, tremendous Polite way of saying "really fat." "I never would have thought that a man of such tremendous girth could be such a . . . creative and sensuous lover," Felicity lies after shagging Fat Bastard so that she can place a homing device in his butt cleavage.

glasses Instrument used to aid vision; spectacles. Austin's glasses have a special function enabling him to increase their magnification, which he does to more closely examine a photograph of himself frozen in his cryogenic chamber. It is thus that he can clearly see the hole drilled in his chamber through which Fat Bastard stole his mojo.

go A sexual encounter. When Felicity sticks a homing device in Fat Bastard's butt cleavage after they have sex, he thinks she is actually indicating her readiness for another sexual encounter. "Frisky, are we?" he asks. "Alright, let's have another go!"

Groovy boy Felicity's complimentary description of Austin.

group therapy See **familial relations, strained.**

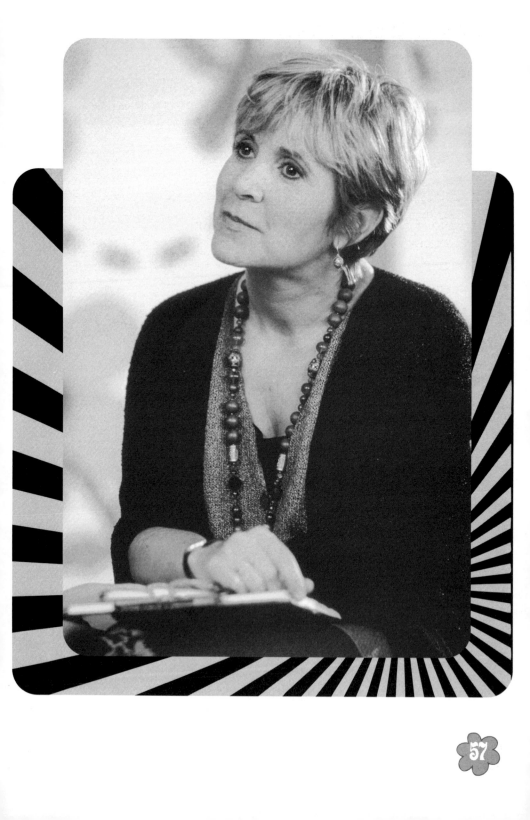

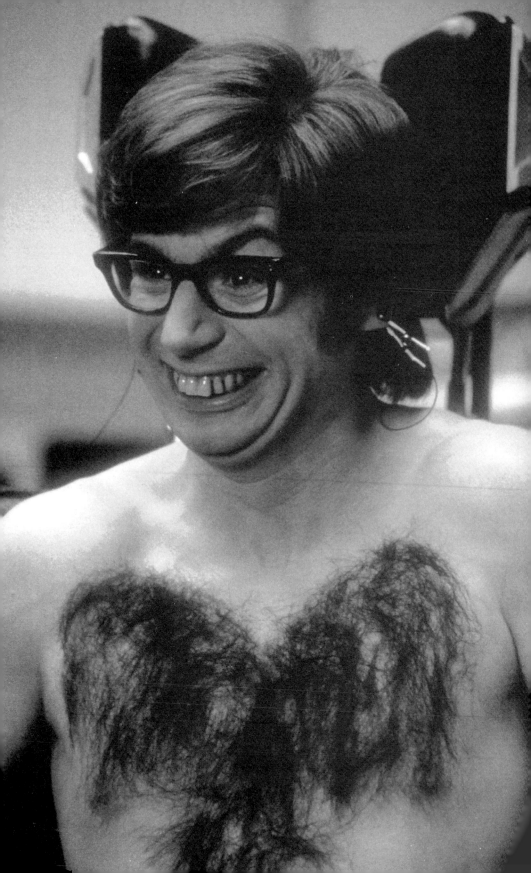

CRIKEY, I've Lost My MOJO!

hairy Descriptive term for the hirsute Austin. Ivana Humpalot, in her Russian accent, notes he is "Hairy, like animal." She also calls him "monkey man." Alotta Fagina observes he is a "silly, hairy little man."

ham sandwich After he has been reanimated from his cryogenically frozen state, Austin learns that eating one was the apparent cause of death of singer Mama Cass.

heinie Butt; bum; ass; tuchus; rear end; hindquarters; buttocks; behind; pants pillow; backside; bottom; bucket; mud flaps; derriere; buns; end; fanny; tush; posterior; tushy; seat; cheeks; dumper; trouser cakes; also, homonymic nickname for Heineken, a Dutch beer, which Austin serves at his party in 1969. When Austin warns an attractive woman to "Get your hand off my Heinie!" he is referring not to his behind but to his beer.

Hell Nether realm of Lucifer where people go when they die and where, Dr. Evil warns Austin, they will meet again.

helmets, meat Hard, protective headwear fashioned from meat products. Dr. Evil recalls that, as a child, he would make meat helmets in the spring.

Henchman Training Seminar Three-week course taken by those who desire to receive full henchman training. Graduates, according to Dr. Evil, receive "a certificate and everything."

Hendrix, Jimi See **"People I Know" list.**

Her Majesty's Vegas Tours See **bus, double-decker tourist.**

Herr Doktor
Teutonic title of respect that the German-speaking Frau Farbissina employs with Dr. Evil.

hipster, aging
Dr. Evil's stinging condemnation of Austin's life and lifestyle. In the closing moments of the first film, when the pair face off in a dramatic confrontation, Evil taunts Austin, "There"s nothing more pathetic than an aging hipster."

homing device
See **cleavage, butt.**

hop on the good foot and do the bad thing
A sexual encounter; a romp; a shag.

Hot Pockets
Microwavable dough filled with various tasty fillings. Dr. Evil tries to break the ice of his and Frau Farbissina's postcoital awkward moment by suggesting that Frau "Try the Hot Pockets – they're breathtaking."

Human Organ Trafficking
One of Virtucon's three secret projects, along with Project Vulcan and a Carrot Top Movie.

human shield
Though Robin Swallows is in on the plot to murder Austin, she ends up taking the firepower meant for him when he uses her as a human shield. She takes a knife in the back, bullets fired from a machine gun, and a bazooka shell; gets blasted out of Austin's second-story flat through a plate-glass window with Austin; and cushions Austin's fall when they land on the sidewalk down below.

Humpalot, Ivana
Russian spy, paid by Dr. Evil.

Independence Day *See* **footage.**

inner monologue Device in theater and film by which a character conveys his inner thoughts to the audience, allowing them to better grasp a plot twist or a motivation. Austin realizes too late that one side effect of the postcryogenic reanimation process is his loss of the ability to have an inner monologue. Thus, when he first meets Vanessa and says to himself, "I'll bet she shags like a minx," she – along with everyone else in the room – can and does hear him.

insolence Rude (some might say "uppity") behavior usually exhibited by the young or immature to an authority figure. When Dr. Evil was insolent as a young child, he was placed in a burlap bag and beaten with reeds. "Pretty standard, really," he recalls. Later, we learn that Dr. Evil has had his and Scott's therapy group liquidated "because they were insolent." Also, it is later divulged that Number 2's insolence once cost him a spell in the fiery pit.

instinct When it comes to the spy game, Austin reveals, "it's all instinct." Of course, he says this as he pours himself a nice, tall sample of Fat Bastard's stool.

interdecade dating Problem faced by 1960s Felicity and 1990s Austin.

interrogations, irritating Mustafa so dislikes questions that, when he is asked a question two times, he'll just provide a truthful answer, loyalty be damned. "I can't stand to be asked the same question twice," he reveals. "It just irritates me."

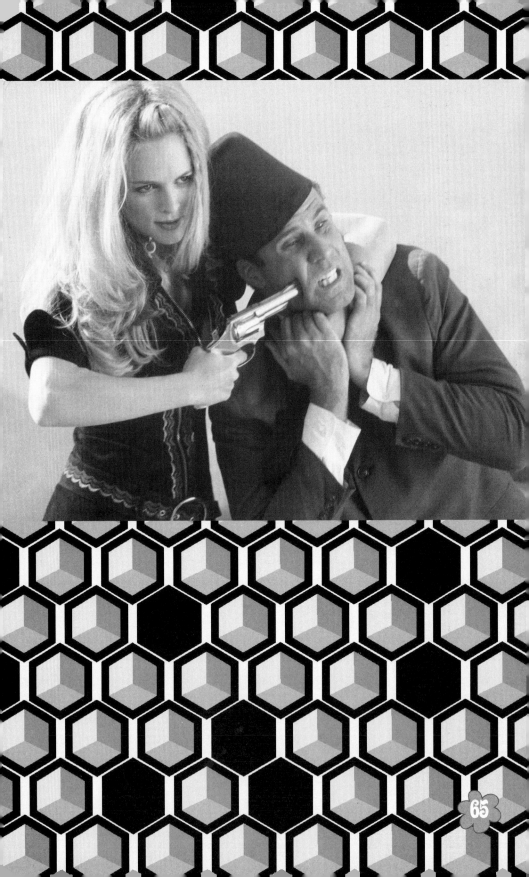

65

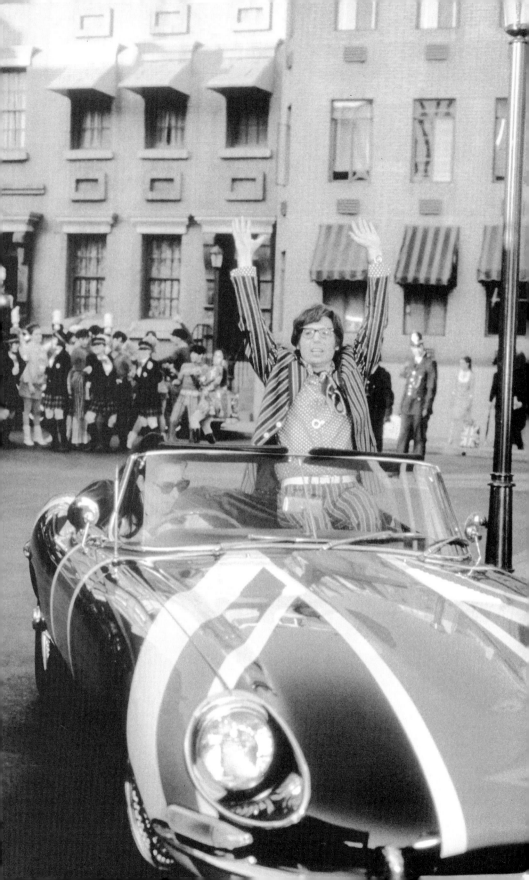

Jack of Clubs Fourth-highest ranked card in the suit of clubs. In a swinging Las Vegas montage, the face of the Jack of Clubs belongs to none other than Austin Powers.

jagoff Possible corruption of "jack off." An insult Scott Evil hurls at a Klansman during a taping of *The Jerry Springer Show.*

Jaguar XKE convertible, 1967 Austin's Union Jack–emblazoned sportscar. In the second film, the car's make has been renamed Shaguar.

jail cell Room used to detain prisoners. The jail cell in Dr. Evil's secret hollowed-out volcano lair, built to house Austin and Felicity, does not have a door.

Japanese sociopolitics While attending to Austin in her hot tub and talking about the importance of gender in Japanese society, Alotta Fagina notes that, "In Japan, men come first and women come second." Austin replies devilishly, "Or sometimes not at all."

Jerry Maguire See "Show me the money."

Jerry Springer Show, The Daytime television program hosted by former mayor of Cincinnati Jerry Springer. The show broke away for the rest of the daytime pack by regularly incorporating slugfests, nudity, and humiliations into its mix. *The Jerry Springer Show* arranges a surprise reunion between Dr. Evil and his son, Scott, in an episode titled "My father is evil and wants to take over the world."

Joplin, Janis *See "People I Know" list.*

jubblies Breasts. When Fembots tried to kill Austin, he explains to Vanessa, "smoke came out of their jubblies."

judo Martial art that emphasizes the use of quick movements in which Austin and both generations of Kensington women are expert. Austin's well-placed judo kick to the body of Frau Farbissina prevents her from aiming Dr. Evil's giant laser at Washington, D.C., and instead fires a painful laser shot directly into the crotch of Dr. Evil's Bob's Big Boy rocket.

"Jumpin' German Jesus!" Exclamation of frustration used by the president of the United States when he learns he must pay Dr. Evil blackmail money.

Jungle Boy Nickname Vanessa has for Austin, perhaps due to his penchant for uttering Tarzan-like yells during their lovemaking.

Jurgen One of Dr. Evil's henchmen who is eventually sent into the fiery pit.

kabuki *See* **United Nations' Secret Meeting Room.**

kamikaze bride Term used by Dr. Evil to describe Vanessa the Fembot when it is revealed that she is actually a ticking time bomb in human form.

Kensington, Mrs. Mother of Vanessa Kensington and, so it seems, a former object of Austin's desire in the 1960s. "She was very groovy," Austin tells Vanessa, but "that train has sailed."

Kensington, Vanessa Top British agent and daughter of Mrs. Kensington.

WOULD YOU FANCY A SHAG?

knickers British for "underwear." Austin's ultrasexy Union Jack knickers help him defeat the Fembots.

knock-knock joke Classic joke form, requiring two individuals to execute it properly, in which the first

person knocks on an imaginary door and the second person inquires who might be at the door. At this point in the joke, the first person gives some (usually nonsensical) name. The second person ordinarily repeats the name and adds the word "who," as if to inquire what the person's last name might be, whereupon the first person moves in for the laugh and delivers the comic punch line, usually a pun involving the name he has supplied. At one point, Dr. Evil initiates this classic joke form with his son, Scott, by leading him with a "Knock knock." Scott replies, quite properly, "Who's there?" and Dr. Evil abandons form and simply says "Sshhh!"

knotted rope Rope used for climbing or descending. A lantern-lit view into Austin and Felicity's tent, showing only their silhouetted figures, makes it seem as if Felicity, when she is pulling a knotted rope out of Austin's suitcase, is actually pulling it out of his mud flaps.

Kreplachistan Former Soviet Republic in either Eastern Europe or Central Asia, the nuclear warheads of which are vulnerable to the whims of Dr. Evil. He is able to hijack one of their nuclear warheads for his Project Vulcan. Kreplach are also Jewish dumplings, usually served in soup.

Ku Klux Klan White supremacist organization whose members wear fashionable white hoods and sheets. Also known as the KKK. A representative from the KKK and his son are featured on *The Jerry Springer Show* episode titled "My Father Is Evil and Wants to Take Over the World," which also features a surprise reunion between Dr. Evil and his son, Scott.

lard, tub of Usually used to describe an enormously
fat fellow. "When you get to be a tub of lard such as
myself, you learn how to pleasure a woman," says Fat
Bastard. "I mean, *really* pleasure a woman."

laser Destructive device often employed by ruthless,
megalomaniacal, despotic figures in science-fiction
films, the utilization of which usually means murder and
mayhem. It can also remove warts. Dr. Evil's diabolical

plan for liquidating Austin and Vanessa is to feed them to sharks who have laser beams attached to their heads "so they can enjoy a hot meal."

laser, giant Dr. Evil places a laser "powerful enough to destroy every city on the planet" on the moon, allowing him to turn the moon into his own personal Death Star and extort money from whomever he chooses. Mini-Me seems to have an unusual sexual fixation with the laser; at one point, when Dr. Evil notices Mini-Me humping the device, he asks his monstrous sidekick, "Why don't you and the laser get a frickin' room? Honestly."

laser cutting See **Reanimation Process.**

lava lamp A 1960s-era artificial light source in which a working lamp also houses flowing molten goo visible through its transparent stem. Also, entertainment for thoroughly wasted stoners. Austin had one in his old shag pad before Reg got rid of it.

lazy-eyed psycho How Scott Evil refers to his father, Dr. Evil, in one of their first encounters.

THE KEY TO LIFE IS TO ROTATE YOUR VICES.

L'chaim Hebrew for "To Life," "L'chaim" is a traditional Jewish toast. In the lobby of Austin's honeymoon hotel, a mohel and a rabbi seem to be performing a circumcision suspiciously close to a bare-bottomed Austin, but it is then revealed that they are actually cutting the tip off a beef tenderloin, at which point everyone yells, "L'chaim!" *See* "**Clinky**"; **mohel.**

lemur Small mammal native to the African savanna, according to Austin. On a photo shoot, Austin asks various fashion models to "be a lemur, baby!"

Liberace Legendary torch-song singer, pianist, and closet homosexual. Austin only learns that Liberace was gay while watching a videotape of historic events that he missed while he was cryogenically frozen. "I didn't see that one coming," he admits.

license plate Means of identification on an automobile. The license plate on Austin's 1967 Jaguar XKE convertible reads SWINGER.

liquidate To eliminate; murder. Number 2 expresses concern at one point that the rate at which Dr. Evil "liquidate[s] henchmen far exceeds our ability to replace them." Also, what the U.S. government does to its gold reserve supply at Fort Knox in order to get Dr. Evil his blackmail money.

liquid-hot magma Molten hot rock from within the earth's core. Dr. Evil delights in sadistically letting the words hang on his lips as he promises that, once his Project Vulcan is unleashed, the liquid-hot magma will destroy the earth.

love that dare not speak its name, the

Homosexuality. Frau Farbissina claims to have embraced
the love that dare not speak its name when she introduces
Dr. Evil to her lover, Unibrau, whom she met on the LPGA tour.

low-level functionary

Unimportant pawn in
someone else's game. This is what Mustafa claims to be
when he is cross-examined by Austin and Felicity.

LPGA Tour

The golfing events that comprise the Ladies Professional Golf Association's annual schedule. *See* **Unibrau.**

lucky charm

Talisman thought to bring good fortune. Dr. Evil's hitman Patty O'Brien is sure to always leave one behind every time he strangles a victim with his lucky-charm bracelet.

luge

Winter sport in which a contestant lies flat on his back on a sled and careens down an icy race course for a competitive time. In a group therapy session, Dr. Evil fondly reminisces about his childhood luge lessons.

lunar landing

Historic achievement of U.S. space program, which in the summer of 1969 saw a three-man U.S. astronaut crew land on the moon. Austin only learns of this event twenty-eight years later while watching a videotape of historic events that he missed while he was cryogenically frozen. But later, thanks to time travel, he and Felicity replace the mission's original astronauts.

lung

See **O-ring.**

Macarena
Faddish Latin American dance popular in the mid 1990s. Dr. Evil demonstrates his knowledge of the dance in an effort to prove to his son, Scott, that he's "hip."

machine-gun jubblies
Machine guns hidden in the mammary glands (jubblies) of Fembots. When Vanessa realizes that her Fembot cover has been blown, the tips of her lethal machine-gun jubblies protrude from her breasts, a sign Austin initially interprets as evidence that the room temperature has gotten significantly chillier.

male symbol Circle with an arrow pointing to the upper right from about one o'clock. It is both the symbol for the planet Mars and is generally recognized as a symbol representative of the male gender. Austin has a silver medallion of this male symbol kept among his valuables while he is frozen cryogenically. The male symbol also adorns his business card and is on the wallpaper of his private jet.

mallet A lantern-lit view into Austin and Felicity's tent, showing only their silhouetted figures, makes it seem as if Felicity, when she is trying to shove a tennis racket into Austin's suitcase by smacking it with a mallet, is actually smacking it deep into his ass. "You've got this packed really tight," she notes.

massage Rubbing of a person's muscles or tissues for therapeutic or pleasurable purposes. According to Felicity, Austin's massages are world famous.

matador See **United Nations' Secret Meeting Room.**

May 25, 1969 Date to which Dr. Evil travels back in time. Also the date on which Fat Bastard steals Austin's mojo while the superagent is cryogenically frozen.

meat and two bits One of the many nicknames Austin has conferred on his genitalia.

ménage à trois French for "household for three," an arrangement or scenario in which three people have a

simultaneous physical sexual encounter. Also, the fantasy of every single heterosexual man in the world. When Past Austin and Future Austin get an eyeful of one another, the subject immediately springs to mind. "Say, what's the policy on ménage à trois?" asks Past Austin.

Meow Mix
A cat food so popular, cats ask for it by name. Dr. Evil sings an extended dance-club mix of the brand's jingle while trying to get Mr. Bigglesworth's attention.

metal detector
See **coins.**

Ming Tea
The name of Austin's pop band, with which he performs the song "BBC."

Mini-Me
Dr. Evil's clone, who is one-eighth his size. He shares all of Evil's mannerisms, including a predilection for biting his pinky in sheer diabolical delight. He sits to Dr. Evil's right in meetings.

Mini-Mr. Bigglesworth
Mr. Bigglesworth's bald kittenlike clone, identical to him in every way except for his smaller size.

Ministry of Defense (M.O.D.)
London-based department of the British government charged with monitoring and dealing with Dr. Evil. M.O.D. housed a frozen Austin in a cryogenic chamber in its London-based Cryogenic Storage Center.

mohel
(pronounced MOYLE) In Judaism, one who performs ritual circumcisions on a male child, eight days after the child's birth. See **L'chaim.**

mojo
A bodily secretion produced more rapidly and more effectively in Austin Powers than in the average of the male species. When Austin works his mojo, he can get virtually any woman he wants. "The life force," observes Dr. Evil in a mojo-inspired soliloquy, "libido, the 'right stuff.' What the French call a certain 'I don't know what.' In the sixties, everyone had mojo." Dr. Evil steals Austin's mojo, leaving him powerless—sexually and otherwise. See **cross-mojination.**

"mojo's working overtime, my"
Horny. When Austin realizes he doesn't need his mojo to shag, he is ready to have a "go" with Felicity. "My mojo's working overtime, baby!" he says. "How about a quick knee-trembler?"

"mongoose to my snake"
What Austin is to Dr. Evil, according to the latter. Then he thinks it might be the other way around. "Either way, it's bad," he says. "I don't know animals."

Monkey Man
An affectionate nickname for Austin, given to him by Ivana Humpalot. Most likely, the name derives from Austin's abundance of body hair.

monster, little How Scott describes Mini-Me after the psychopathic clone puts roadkill in Scott's bed.

moon A planetary-like entity that orbits the earth, controls its tides, and dictates the behavior of werewolves. Also home to Dr. Evil's moon base, from which he hopes to direct at the earth a laser "powerful enough to destroy every city on the planet."

Morse code A language of dots and dashes (for print) or long and short sounds (for audio), used primarily to communicate secret messages between parties. Dr. Evil relays the following Morse code message to his son, Scott: "Sshhh! Sshh-Sshhh. Sshh-Sshhhhh-Sshh. Sshh-Sshhh!" After pausing for a moment to read an imaginary piece of paper, he says, "Let me decipher. . . . It says 'Sshhh!'"

Mummy-Daddy dance Shagging. After he loses his mojo, Austin tells Felicity that he has "forgotten the steps to the Mummy-Daddy dance."

Mustafa The fez-wearing advisor to Dr. Evil who plays a key role in Evil's empire.

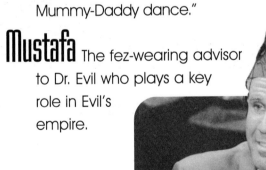

Mustang convertible American-made vehicle driven by
American CIA agent Felicity Shagwell. *See* **product
placement.**

"My Father Is Evil and Wants to Take Over the World"
Episode of *The Jerry Springer Show* on *which* Dr. Evil and
his son, Scott, appear.

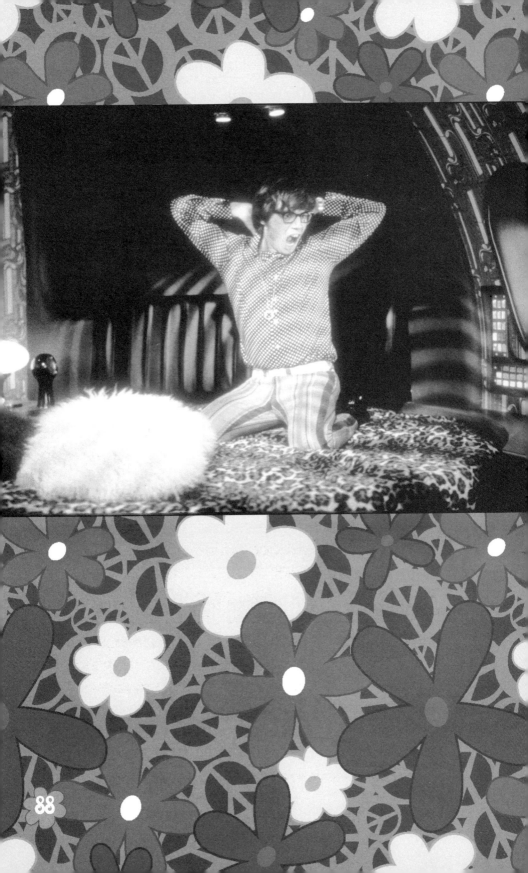

narcissism Excessive self-admiration. Like when one gets the "hots" for oneself. Austin exhibits narcissistic tendencies, admiring himself as a "sexy bitch" in mirrors or photographs; admiring his own naked body frozen on ice ("Look at me. I'm striking, aren't I? I'm downright handsome!"); and confusingly appreciating his actual self in the flesh from ten minutes earlier. Number 2 also exhibits narcissistic tendencies, at one point sleeping with a version of himself from thirty years earlier.

narcolepsy Condition characterized by brief attacks

of deep sleep. Dr. Evil's father, it is learned in a group therapy session, suffered from low-grade narcolepsy. *See* **buggery**.

Nehru jacket Collarless jacket made popular in 1960s by first prime minister of independent India, Jawaharlal Nehru, and favored by Dr. Evil.

Nelson, Willie Famous American country singer. When Dr. Evil's moon ship in the shape of a flying penis passes over a Willie Nelson concert, a guitarist shouts, "Willie!" He is not alerting the concertgoers to Dr. Evil's ship, but rather is trying to get Willie Nelson's attention.

"Nerd Alert" What Austin yells when he notices that Vanessa has, in her anal-retentive manner, carefully labeled everything in her suitcase.

nerve gas One gas released – probably among others – by Fat Bastard when he plays bagpipes in the M.O.D. cryogenic freezing room, thus knocking unconscious the other soldiers standing guard over Austin's frozen body.

NORAD North American Aerospace Defense Command, a binational command involving the United States and Canada that provides warning of missile and air attacks against both of its member nations. NORAD's Combat Operations Center is the first intelligence unit to notice Dr. Evil's reentry into the earth's atmosphere.

November 11, 1967 Date on which Austin enters his cryogenic chamber. He subsequently remains frozen for thirty years.

nuclear war *See* **things that scare Austin Powers, two.**

Number 2 Dr. Evil's second-in-command. Wears an eye patch over his right eye, though the vision in that eye does not seem to be impaired. Number 2 runs Virtucon in Dr. Evil's absence, helping it grow into a multibillion-dollar company.

numb-nuts An insult. Scott Evil call his father "numb-nuts" when Dr. Evil mistakes "billions" for being greater in value than "trillions."

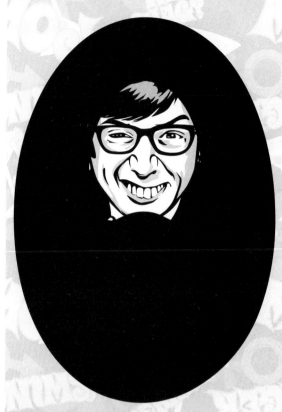

O'Brien, Patty *See* lucky charms.

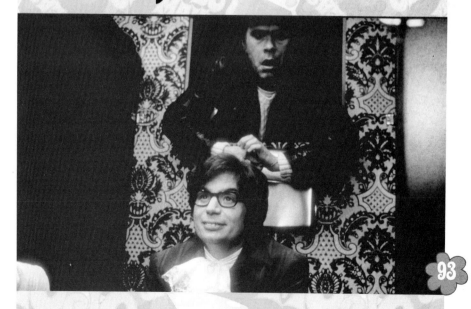

"Oh, Behave" Austin's multisituational exclamation, usually used to coyly fan the flames of sexual tension, even if the tension is only imagined on his part.

oil refinery Plant that processes oil for distribution. Virtucon owns an oil refinery in Seattle, Washington.

oil spill Accidental – and wasteful – loss of oil, usually by a ship at sea, due to negligence or disaster. A mojo-less Austin reluctantly consents to give the insistent Felicity a massage, but when she unties the strap of her sexy dress, he loses control and accidentally spurts way too much oil.

old shag pad Austin's affectionate nickname for his former 1960s residence on Carnaby Street in London.

Oompa-Loompa vibe, creepy Aura given off by Mini-Me. Oompa-Loompas are the small freaks of nature from the movie *Willy Wonka and the Chocolate Factory*.

Operation Wang Chung Name Scott Evil sarcastically suggests his father use for his deadly laser endeavor after Dr. Evil has decided on the ridiculous name The Alan Parsons Project.

O-ring Rubber ring that is used to keep fluid out of a valve or joint. O-rings are a critical part of any space shuttle operation. When Austin is struggling in the bathroom with Patty O'Brien, a gregarious Texan stranger thinks he's passing a difficult bowl movement. Offering advice, he tells him to relax – otherwise, "You're gonna blow out your O-ring, drop a lung."

ozone layer Thin layer of protection in the stratosphere that protects living things from the sun's ultraviolet rays. Dr. Evil plans on punching a hole in this layer unless the United Nations coughs up ransom money – that is, until Number 2 informs him that a hole in the ozone layer already exists.

Paddington Station Central train station in London where Felicity's homing device tracks down Fat Bastard in a public bathroom.

Paris talk How the under-educated Scott Evil refers to the French language.

Parsons Project, The Alan Name Dr. Evil gives to his Death Star laser endeavor. After all, he notes, the laser "was invented by the noted Cambridge physicist Dr. Parsons."

Past Austin One of the many Austins. This particular Austin is the one that "saves the world" on Dr. Evil's moon base, while Future Austin saves Felicity.

penicillin See **clap, the**.

penis Austin has his own personal arsenal of names for his genitalia, including "bits and pieces," "twig and berries," "wedding tackle," and "meat and two bits." When aroused, he might well say, "Hello, Vicar." And occasionally he might point out that "I like to give my undercarriage a 'how's your father.'"

penis-enlarger pump, Swedish-made Device used

to enhance the size and stature of the male sex organ. Though Austin vigorously denies ownership of the Swedish-made penis-enlarger pump, it is one of items kept in storage for him while he is cryogenically frozen. The tool later helps him overcome Asian strongman Random Task.

"People I Know" list List of Austin's friends who die while he is cryogenically frozen: Mama Cass, Jerry Garcia, Janis Joplin, and Jimi Hendrix.

"personal, This time it's" Declaration made by Dr. Evil about his ongoing epic struggle with Austin after Dr. Evil reveals his Alan Parsons Project to the president of the United States.

petting zoo, evil Gentle, peaceful place where young children can interact with domesticated and farm animals. When Scott Evil mentions in group therapy that he might want to work in a petting zoo, Dr. Evil holds out hope that it will be an "evil petting zoo."

PG-13 Rating given to some movies by the Motion Picture Association of America, in which parents are "strongly cautioned," as "some material may be inappropriate for children under thirteen."

piano Instrument on which Dr. Evil plays the Joan Osborne classic "What If God Was One of Us?" in a duet with Mini-Me.

pigs, capitalist Derogatory term often used to demean acquisitive denizens of the West. After Austin is reanimated from his frozen cryogenic state, Basil introduces him to a Russian general, telling the just-unfrozen superagent that the "Cold War is over." This prompts Austin to believe that Russia and the East have triumphed. "Those capitalist pigs will pay for their crimes, eh, comrades?" offers Austin. After he is informed that the West has actually won the Cold War, Austin offers a sheepish "Yay, capitalism!" cheer.

pills Testicles. When Felicity kicks Fat Bastard in the testicles, Austin chides her, "I don't care if he is a bastard, you don't kick a man in the pills. It just ain't cricket, baby."

"Pleasure, The" Having a shag with Austin. When fashion model Rebecca Romijn introduces herself to Austin, she says, "I don't believe I've had the pleasure." "Of course you haven't had 'The Pleasure,'" he retorts devilishly. "We just met, baby, yeah."

poetry Rhythmic, metrical writing composed to produce an emotional response. Austin recites the following poem after passing wind in Alotta Fagina's hot tub: "Pardon me for being rude/It was not me it was my food/It just popped up to say hello/And now it's gone back down below."

Powers, Austin

International Man of Mystery. His former partner, Mrs. Kensington, may have said it most succinctly:

AUSTIN POWERS

Austin is "the ultimate gentleman spy, irresistible to women, deadly to his enemies, and legend in his own time." His teeth aren't so good, however.

Powers' Kama Sutra, Austin Book offering Austin's perspective on the ancient Hindu text that teaches various positions for lovemaking. Austin's includes such innovative techniques as The Wheelbarrow, The Praying Donkey, and The Chinese Shag Swing.

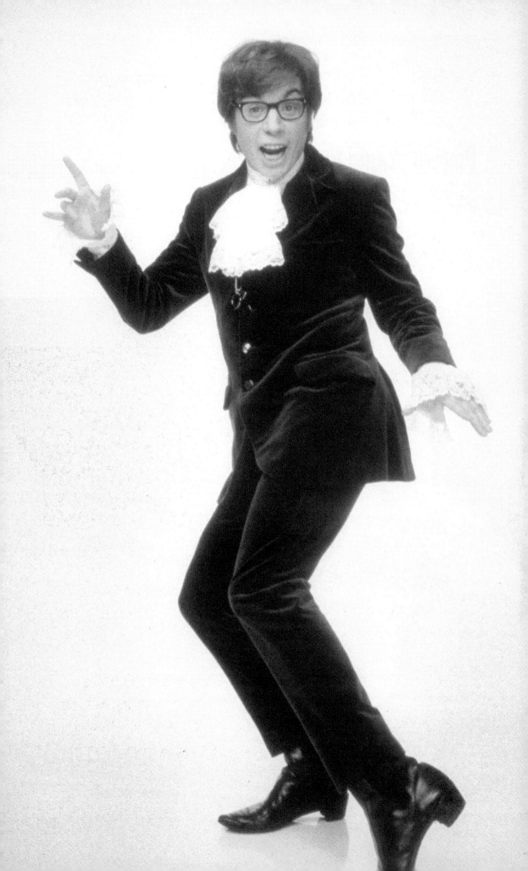

prank What Dr. Evil calls the incident in which Mini-Me maliciously put roadkill in Scott Evil's bed.

preemptive sshhh! *See* **Sshhh!.**

privates Soldiers who hold the rank of private in the army. When Dr. Evil's moon ship, which looks like a flying penis, passes over an army base, a sergeant shouts, "Privates!" It seems as if he is alerting them to Dr. Evil's ship, but he is actually calling for their attention.

private session

In Austin's photography vernacular, a "private session" is a special one-on-one photo shoot. A sexual liaison is also implied. When international fashion supermodel Rebecca Romijn believes they have plans with Austin on a given night, he disappoints the two of them, telling them he and Ivana Humpalot "are going to have a private session."

private time Euphemism for sex. After drinking Austin's mojo, Dr. Evil dismisses all of his associates from a board meeting – except Frau Farbissina, with whom he wants to "get it on" – by saying, "Okay, everyone, private time."

product placement Process by which producers of a film or television show collect payments from manufacturers in exchange for prominently featuring said manufacturers' products in their films or shows. For example, *The Spy Who Shagged Me* prominently features such multinational products as Heineken beer, Starbucks coffee, Bob's Big Boy, Macintosh computers, Phillips TV, and a Ford Mustang.

Project Vulcan Code name for Dr. Evil's plan to drill a hole into the center of the earth, explode a Kreplachistani nuclear warhead, and force all the world's volcanoes to explode at once. It is, Austin learns, just one of Virtucon's three dastardly projects, the other two being Human Organ Trafficking and a Carrot Top Movie.

prostitution World's oldest profession. Prostitutes, usually women, ply their trade by performing acts of a sexual nature for cash. Dr. Evil's mother was a fifteen-year-old prostitute named Chloe who had webbed feet.

psychopathy Mental disorder characterized by extremely antisocial behavior. Mini-Me seems to suffer from this malady: He does not speak, so much as grunt and snarl, and is only too eager to murder, take over the world, etc. He especially seems to have it in for Scott Evil, his rival for the affection of Dr. Evil. Scott is rightfully convinced that Mini-Me is after him. "He's crazy! He wants to kill me! He's totally evil!" warns Scott. "I know," says the unsympathetic Dr. Evil. "He makes me so proud."

pulleys, elaborate set of Stunned by the knowledge that Felicity has shagged Fat Bastard, Austin is as puzzled as to *how* she did it as to why. "The sheer mechanics of it are mind-boggling. Did you use an elaborate set of pulleys? A block and tackle? A hoist, perhaps?"

pump sneakers Genus of athletic shoe unique to the mid 1990s; wearers "pump" their shoes with air to secure a better fit. Austin mistakenly pumps his sneaker until it explodes in his face. *See* **penis-enlarger pump.**

punji sticks Deadly, pointy sticks. As part of his elaborate escape plan from Dr. Evil's secret hollowed-out volcano-lair jail cell, Austin suggests that Felicity "dig a pit and line it with makeshift punji sticks, made from sharpened toothbrushes."

pussy Another name for a domesticated cat. See
  Bigglesworth, Mr.

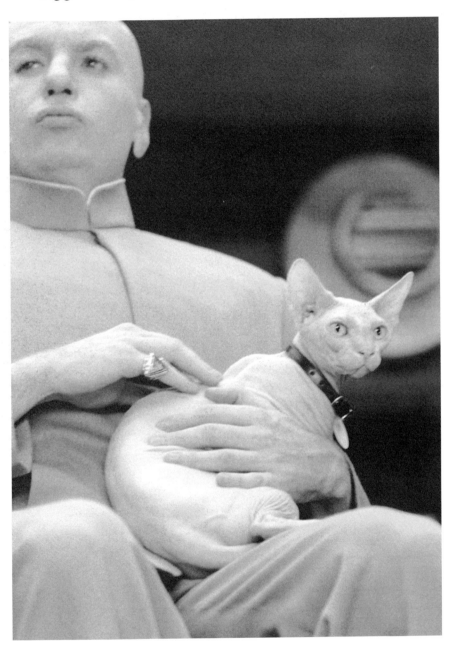

quasifuturistic clothes Shiny silver outfits given

to Austin and Vanessa by Dr. Evil when he captures

them in his underground lair. There's a little Bob Mackie

in Dr. Evil – he designed the adorable little outfits himself.

Queen Elizabeth II Current ruling monarch of the United Kingdom. Basil announces at the end of the first film that Austin is to be knighted by the queen.

Quotations from Chairman Mao Tse-tung

Little red book that was required reading in Maoist-era China. When Dr. Evil's moon ship passes over a Chinese Communist classroom, a student named Wang is clutching his little red copy of *Quotations from Chairman Mao Tse-tung.*

Random Task
Dr. Evil's hulking Asian manservant. Deadly with a black loafer, Random Task closely resembles Odd Job, a hulking Asian manservant from the James Bond films who was deadly with his hat.

rap music
Genre of popular music characterized by impressive wordplay, lengthy narratives, and a hip-hop beat. Dr. Evil tries his hand at the rap game in a lyrical terrain that seems to focus mainly on his disdain for his son, Scott, and his adoration of his monstrous little clone, Mini-Me. Sample lyrics: "I hoped Scott would look up to me/Run the business of the family/Head an evil empire just like dear old dad/Give him ma love and the things he never had. . . . But Scott rejected me/C'est la vie."

Reanimation Process

This complex, five-stage process is utilized to bring a person who has been in a cryogenically frozen state back to life. If you happen to stumble across a cryogenically frozen individual, now you can bring him back to life in your home using the following five steps:

Stage 1: Laser Cutting (Lasers chip away the ice blocks in which an individual is frozen.)

Stage 2: Warm Liquid Goo (Individual is placed in a large vat of warm liquid goo to help him thaw.)

Stage 3: Reanimation (Formerly frozen individual shows signs of life and consciousness.)

Stage 4: Cleansing (Individual is bathed in hot, soapy liquid.)

Stage 5: Evacuation (Individual empties the long-stored urine from his kidneys or, in layman's terms, "takes a leak.")

refractory period

Passing interval after a penis ejaculates before it is ready for another "go." Video of a scientific diagram of a penis in the refractory period metaphorically represents Austin's loss of his mojo. Unfortunately, it occurs at a most inopportune time – when he is in bed with Ivana Humpalot.

remote control After many hours of lovemaking, Vanessa indicates that she does not want to shag any longer, so Austin settles for a movie. He picks up a remote control and presses the Fast Forward, Play, Rewind, Mute, and SAP buttons, which somehow get crossed with Vanessa's Fembot wiring, causing her to mimic each of the remote's functions. It is thus revealed to Austin that his beloved wife, "the woman who taught me the beauty of monogamy," is a Fembot. Austin later tests Felicity while she is sleeping by pointing a remote control at her to see if she, too, is a Fembot.

right stuff, the See **mojo**

ri-goddamn-diculous Exclamation of frustation. Confused by the simultaneous appearance of Past Austin and Future Austin, Dr. Evil reaches his boiling point. "This is ri-goddamn-diculous!" he tells his henchmen. "Kill them both!"

"Rip-off!" Scott, pretending to sneeze, actually yells "rip-off!" when his father announces his intentions to place his giant, deadly laser on the moon and then rename the astral body Death Star. Scott is referring to the fact that the name Death Star has already been used in the *Star Wars* films.

Rita One of Dr. Evil's henchwomen. We see her name on Dr. Evil's deadly control panel, and then, when Dr. Evil presses the RITA button, we see a woman in a military/meter maid uniform tumble backward into the fiery pit.

Riviera, French Chi-chi vacation spot in the south of France. Place where Austin and Vanessa spend their honeymoon, until she blows up. The hotel in which Austin and Vanessa reside during their stay in Las Vegas, by the way, is the Riviera Hotel.

roadkill *See* **prank.**

Romijn, Rebecca Famous fashion model who poses for Austin on a photo shoot. He is not sure if she is a Russian spy.

Royal Canadian Mounted Police *See* **United Nations' Secret Meeting Room.**

SORRY I FARTED.

sailors Those whose occupation requires them to work on seagoing vessels. In Austin's mind, no other members of the world's workforce need to use prophylactics during the sex act. "Only sailors use condoms," he tells Vanessa when she asks him if he had had safe sex with Alotta Fagina.

salad tongs A scientist picks up Fat Bastard's giant stool with salad tongs and places it in a baggie so that it can later be laboratory tested.

Salvation Army Suspiciously noncombative international unit. The militant wing of the Salvation Army is headed by Frau Farbissina, one of Dr. Evil's top advisors.

sausages, string of "Something smells terrible!" Felicity groans. A lantern-lit view into Austin and Felicity's tent, showing only silhouetted figures, makes it seem as if Felicity, when she is pulling a string of sausages out of Austin's suitcase, is actually pulling them out of his derriere. "These have spoiled," she says disgustedly.

schemes, diabolical Malevolent ideas. Every last one of the various evil plans hatched by Dr. Evil, he laments, "has been thwarted by Austin Powers." It is for that reason that Dr. Evil decides to take away Austin's mojo.

Scots Guard A unit of the British army comprising Scottish soldiers. Fat Bastard is a member of the Scots Guard. And an obscenely obese one, at that.

Scott Evil button Controls the seat in which Scott Evil sits in either the Virtucon or Starbucks boardrooms. One time, when Scott tells his dad that his plan for the evening consist of watching a I & A porn film on Skin-a-Max (*see* **titty movie**), Dr. Evil tries to press the Scott Evil button, but is restrained by the searing whip of Frau Farbissina.

scrotum The external pouch of the male genitalia that, traditionally, hold the testes. When Dr. Evil was fourteen, he claims, a Zoroastrian named Vilma ritualistically shaved his testicles. "There's nothing like a shorn scrotum," he remarks. "It's breathtaking, I suggest you try it."

sea bass, ill-tempered, mutated

See **endangered species.**

Sega Popular video game manufacturer. When Dr. Evil is preparing to abandon his underground lair, he asks Scott to hurry along. The younger Evil thereupon asks, "Can I take my Sega?"

shag To boff. To make the beast with two backs. To do the nasty. You know, get down, make love, all that. To engage in sexual intercourse. An all-consuming preoccupation of Austin's.

shagadelic Excellent, wonderful. As when a sommelier might say, "You'll find that our wine list, sir, is most shagadelic."

Shaguar Apparently a late-model sports vehicle produced in small numbers by the Jaguar car company. Austin drives one in 1999.

Shagwell, Felicity American CIA agent. "Shagwell by name," she says as she introduces herself to Austin, "Shag-*very*-well by reputation."

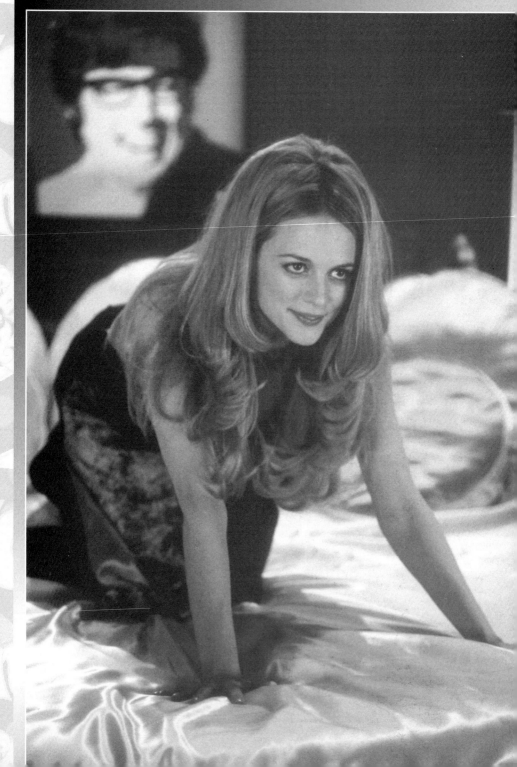

Sherlock Nickname given to Austin by Vanessa after it is revealed that she is a Fembot. It is not exactly what one would call an affectionate nickname, being more along the lines of an insult, actually. Specifically, after Austin shouts "Vanessa, you're a Fembot!" in disbelief, she comes back at him with, "No shit, Sherlock."

shipping mill Virtucon owns one in Texas.

shitter Toilet. Upon meeting Dr. Evil to present him with Austin's mojo, Fat Bastard first demands to know, "Where's your shitter? I've gotta turtle head pokin' out."

shore leave See **clap, the.**

"Show me the money" Shrill, oft-repeated line from the irritating film *Jerry Maguire*. When the president of the United States does not immediately cough up the cash Dr. Evil wants as blackmail in order not to destroy Washington, D.C., Dr. Evil yells, "Show me the money!" When 1999 Dr. Evil is dumbfounded that the 1969 president has no reaction to this, Scott Evil explains that the movie came out in the 1990s, and that the president would have no idea what he is talking about. "It's 1969 – *Jerry Maguire* won't come out for another thirty years, ass."

silver egg space capsule Dr. Evil's silver egg capsule fits neatly inside his Bob's Big Boy rocket.

situation, easily escapable See **death, overly elaborate and exotic.**

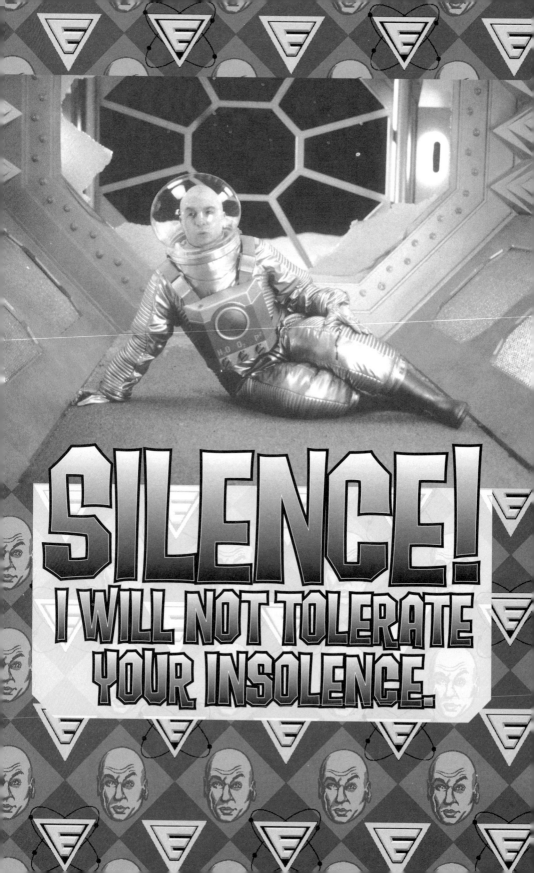

Skin-a-Max Broadcast network that seems to feature a fair number of "T&A" films. At one point, when Dr. Evil asks Scott what his plans for the evening might be, Scott notes that there is "a titty movie on Skin-a-Max."

sleepy Impotent. After he loses his mojo, Austin tells Felicity that "my bits and pieces are sleepy."

Sonny Jim Condescending, derisive name Fat Bastard calls Austin when he steals his mojo. "I got your mojo now, Sonny Jim."

space Part of the universe beyond the earth's stratosphere. This is where Dr. Evil has traveled while cryogenically frozen on at least two occasions, biding his time until he felt it was safe to come back to earth.

Space Needle Tall, renowned, pointless tourist attraction in Seattle, Washington. At the top of the Space Needle is Starbucks World Headquarters, corporate home of Dr. Evil and his colleagues.

spice rack A unit of storage used to hold small bottles of spices. Basil gives a spice rack to Austin and Vanessa as a wedding present, which, when Vanessa holds it up for Austin to see, prompts him to say, "Nice rack."

Spitz Maiden name of Dr. Evil's German spy, Robin Swallows. *See* **Swallows, Robin.**

spuds, boiling Horny. When Austin realizes he doesn't need his mojo to shag, he is ready to have a "go" with Felicity. "Oh hello!" he yells happily. "My spuds are boiling!"

spy game *See* **instinct.**

Sshhh! Exclamation used to urge another person to be quiet. Dr. Evil uses it ad nauseam when Scott advises him to simply shoot Austin and Vanessa with a gun, rather than kill them by feeding them to ill-tempered, mutated sea bass. At first, one "sshhh!" is insufficient. It is followed up by another. Then by a "preemptive sshhh!," which is in turn followed by a "whole bag of sshhh! with your name on it." That in turn is followed by a knock-knock joke in which the person doing the knocking is none other than "Sshhh!"

Starbucks Seattle-based multinational corporation that is slowly strangling the life out of every other coffee manufacturer on the planet. It is revealed that this company is actually owned by Dr. Evil.

Steamroller Testing Facility
When Austin and Vanessa break into a restricted area in the Virtucon campus, they find themselves in the plant's Steamroller Testing Facility. They somehow end up driving a steamroller themselves and, unfortunately, roll over one of Dr. Evil's henchmen, who is unable to get out of the way in time. Don't think Austin is cruel, however. The guy had plenty of time to get out of the way. In fact, the guy could have baked a basket of frickin' brownies in the time he had to get out of the way. He just panicked, is all.

steel mill Virtucon owns one in Cleveland, Ohio.

stick, ugly What Austin says Basil's mother, Mrs. Expostion, looks like she has been beaten with. Austin mistakenly takes her for being a man and subsequently knocks the snot out of the elderly woman with a vicious right uppercut.

St. Ides Malt liquor brand, popular with hip-hop groups and endorsed by such rappers as Ice Cube. Dr. Evil, it seems, is also a loyal patron, as he breaks out a St. Ides forty-ounce during his "private time" with Frau Farbissina.

Stool Sample—Fat Bastard The label on the side of a beaker in which sits Fat Bastard's fecal memento. The giant, revolting turd that Bastard left behind in a Paddington Station toilet is taken to an M.O.D. laboratory where it can be tasted. I mean tested.

straws, grasping at In a last-ditch effort to save his own life after having been shot in the leg by Austin, Dr. Evil tells his adversary that he is his father. When a stunned Austin replies, "Really?" Dr. Evil admits, "No. I can't back that up. I was just grasping at straws. I had nothing."

sugar Austin almost saves himself from taking a sip of the most wretched cup of coffee ever seen in this or any other galaxy by pausing to add sugar. But in the end he only sweetens the ante.

suit, blue crushed-velvet One of the items kept in storage for Austin while he is cryogenically frozen.

suit, hazardous-material Worn by the scientist who carries Fat Bastard's stool out of Paddington Station, to protect himself from any potential life-threatening illnesses.

suit, zip-up During his "private-time" session with Frau Farbissina, Dr. Evil unzips his gray one-piece suit and reveals that, underneath, he wears suspenders and a T-shirt.

sumo wrestler *See* **United Nations' Secret Meeting Room.**

Swallows, Robin German spy working for Dr. Evil. Her maiden name is Spitz. Upon meeting her, Austin asks her, "Well, which is it, baby, Spitz or Swallows?"

Sweet Jay Friend of Scott's who takes him to a video arcade, where they encounter some French hooligans.

Swinger Austin's name for the *Apollo 11* lunar module that he and Felicity land on the moon. "The Swinger has landed," he tells Houston when they touch down. Also, Austin's vanity license plate.

switched on
Excellent. *See* **shagadelic.**

synchronized swimming Summer Olympic sport in which one or more swimmers perform aquatic dance moves in a pool, meant to be executed in synch with a song (usually something from Broadway). While Austin strolls about his honeymoon hotel, quite nude, we think we are about to see his wedding tackle, when he quickly jumps into the hotel pool. When he emerges, he leads eleven synchronized swimmers in an elaborate routine.

syringe Device used in medical procedures to inject or withdraw liquids. Fat Bastard uses a high-tech syringe to steal Austin's mojo while the latter is cryogenically frozen. The syringe has an LED (light-emitting diode) to indicate the amount of mojo in a given source. Green indicates FULL MOJO, red means no JO.

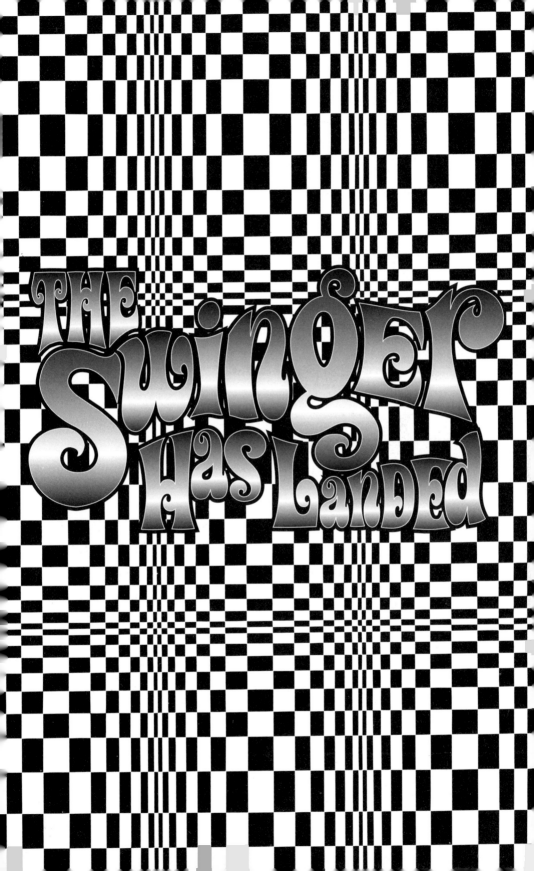

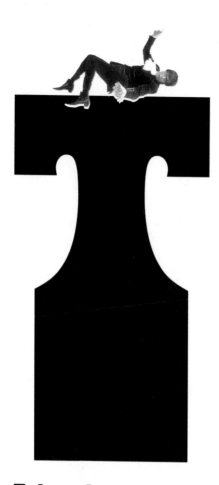

Tab soda Very popular diet soft drink from the 1960s that has since faded from popularity. While catching up on historic events he has missed while being cryogenically frozen for thirty years, Austin drinks about half a case of Tab soda.

"Talk to the hand!" Expression of the 1990s, the meaning of which is roughly equivalent to "Sshhh!" (*see* **bag of sshhh!**). When the 1969 president of the United States protests Dr. Evil's negotiating strategy, Dr. Evil says, "Talk to the hand," to which the president says, "Your hand? Why should I talk to your hand? This guy's a nutbar." To which Dr. Evil says, "Don't go there, girlfriend."

teatime Traditional British snacktime, usually featuring sandwiches, cookies, and of course, tea, served daily around 4 P.M. The 1999 Austin hopes to "go back to the sixties, recharge my mojo, defeat Dr. Evil, and be back in time for tea."

tennis racket See **mallet.**

Thatcher naked on a cold day, Margaret

Former prime minister of the United Kingdom, nude. In an effort to avoid succumbing to the deadly sexual advances of the Fembots, Austin tries to conjure up the least sexually appealing image he can think of.

thin bastard, a What Austin suggests might be living inside of Fat Bastard, trying to get out.

things that scare Austin Powers, two In a plaintive moment, Austin admits that there are two things that scare him. The first is nuclear war; the second is carneys, people who work in carnivals. Austin's fear of the second derives from the fact that these circus folk move like "nomads" and "smell like cabbage."

thrombo A snit; a hissy fit. At one point, Austin pleads with Vanessa, who is jealous of his interest in Alotta Fagina, to pull herself together. "Don't have a thrombo!"

Tiger, Tony the

Cartoon mascot for Kellogg's Frosted Flakes brand cereal, whose most famous schtick has him saying that his cereal is "grrrrr-eat!" When working as a fashion photographer with models, Austin often asks them to pretend they are tigers and, on occasion, even to pretend that they are Tony the Tiger.

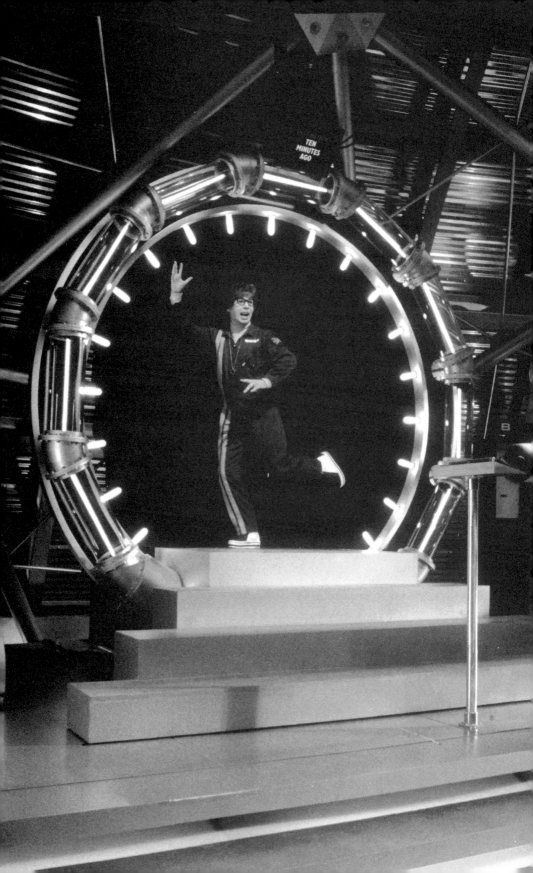

time machine Device used to travel from the present moment into either the past or the future. Both Dr. Evil and the British government seem to have completed time travel technology at the same time, and both use it rather frequently in 1999 to travel to 1969.

time portal Dr. Evil's unnecessarily grandiose word for "time machine." See **time machine.**

titty movie Film in which breasts are bared prominently and frequently. See **Skin-a-Max.**

toilet Depository of the "most disgusting thing I've ever seen," according to Austin, specifically a large Scottish turd. Fat Bastard left his "trophy" behind in a Paddington Station toilet. Toilets play a significant role in Austin's universe: a toilet flushes Mini-Me into outer space, and Patty O'Brien also drowns in a toilet.

toilet, made of solid gold An object of Austin's desire. When he meets a Russian spy for the first time, she divulges that her name is Ivana Humpalot. "And I vanna toilet made of solid gold," Austin replies, "But it's just not in the cards, now, is it?"

tread marks, flaming If a vehicle travels fast enough to leave flaming tread marks, it is probably fast enough to travel through time. See **Volkswagen Beetle, convertible.**

trillions An amount larger than billions. It seems, however, that Dr. Evil has not brushed up on his math skills, and is not aware of that. When Number 2 suggests that Dr. Evil travel back in time to "use your knowledge of the future to play the stock market [so] we could make trillions," Dr. Evil responds, smugly, "Why make trillions when we could make . . . *billions*?" To which Scott Evil says, "A trillion is more than a billion, numb-nuts."

turd, renegade In the bathroom stall next to him, a gregarious Texan stranger hears Austin shouting, "Who does Number 2 work for?" repeatedly. Unaware that Number 2 is the name of Dr. Evil's deputy and that, furthermore, Austin is struggling with Number 2's hired assassin in his stall, the Texan stranger simply believes that Austin has a renegade turd on his hands. So, when Austin demands to know of hitman Patty O'Brien, "Who does Number 2 work for?" the Texan is impressed by Austin's lavatory grit and shouts out encouragement, yelling, "You show that turd who's boss."

turkey leg, huge What Fat Bastard, having just finished making love to Felicity, is eating in bed.

turtle head Presumably the bottom tip of a turd. Upon meeting Dr. Evil to present him with Austin's mojo, Fat Bastard first demands to know, "Where's your shitter? I've gotta turtle head pokin' out."

twig and berries One of the many nicknames Austin has conferred on his genitalia.

Twister Very popular board game from the 1960s and 1970s that physically requires the participants to place their extremities on various colored "spots" on the game board, thus entangling their bodies together. At this point, in their hotel room, Austin and Vanessa are deeply involved in a game of Twister, which ends with the two of them in a heap on the floor after Austin spins a "right hand, green."

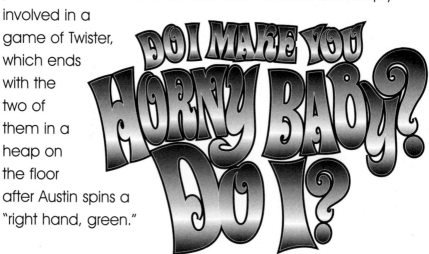

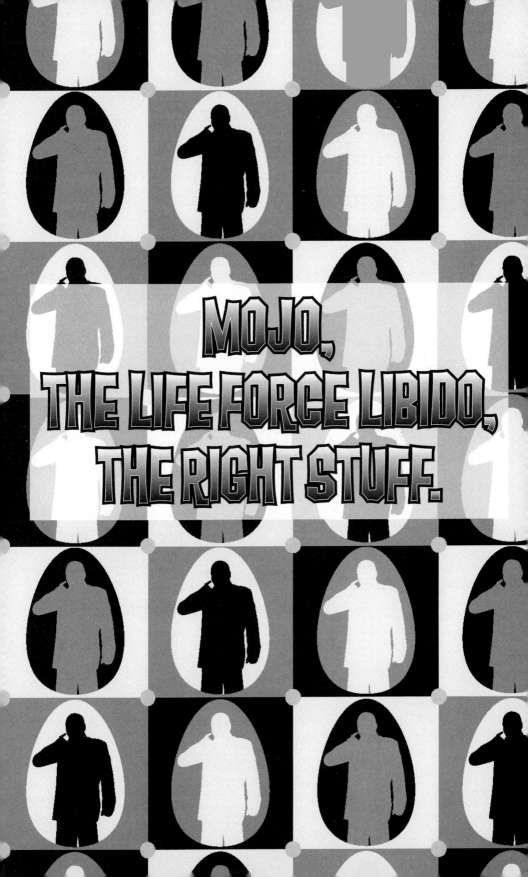

umbrella A lantern-lit view into Austin and Felicity's tent, showing only their silhouetted figures, makes it seem as if Felicity, when she is pulling an umbrella out of Austin's suitcase, is actually pulling it out of his bum. "I'll thank you for not opening that inside," says Austin. "It's bad luck."

umpire Referee of a baseball game. When Dr. Evil's moon ship, which looks like a flying penis, passes over a baseball game, an umpire shouts, "Two balls!" It seems as if he is alerting the crowd to the tail end of Dr. Evil's ship, but he actually is calling out the pitching count.

undercarriage One of the many nicknames Austin has conferred on his genitalia.

underground lair Subterranean, all-purpose laboratory/weapons-storage facility/chalet of any megalomaniacal wing nut worth his salt. Having one is virtually a prerequisite to being considered a respectable adversary of a British superagent.

underwear See **knickers.**

Unibrau Germanic woman who is introduced to Dr. Evil by Frau Farbissina as her lesbian lover. They met on the LPGA Tour. *See* **LPGA.**

Union Jack Flag of the United Kingdom. Austin has a Union Jack emblazoned both on his car and on his knickers.

United Nations' Secret Meeting Room Room (presumed to be in the august international body's New York headquarters, though if we knew the exact location, it wouldn't exactly be a secret, now, would it?) in which a group of typical international diplomatic types – including a sumo wrestler, a matador, a Kabuki dancer, a Beefeater, and a Royal Canadian Mounted Policeman – convene an emergency meeting to hear Dr. Evil reveal the mandate of his Project Vulcan.

Vanilla Ice *See* **Celebrity Vault.**

vet, evil A veterinarian is a doctor who is trained specifically to care for animals. When Scott Evil mentions in group therapy that he likes animals and is considering a career as a veterinarian, Dr. Evil holds out hope that he will practice as an "evil vet." *See* **petting zoo, evil.**

Vicar One of the many nicknames Austin has conferred on his genitalia. As in when he gets aroused, he may say "Hello, Vicar."

Vilma Zoroastrian who, when Dr. Evil was fourteen, ritualistically shaved the young man's testicles.

vinyl album, Burt Bacharach Plays His Hits

See **Bacharach, Burt.**

Virtucon Dr. Evil's company. The "legitimate face of my evil empire," Virtucon was originally known for producing "volatile oil." Thanks to Number 2, Virtucon now owns cable television companies in thirty-eight states, a steel mill in Cleveland, a shipping mill in Texas, an oil refinery in Seattle, and a factory in Chicago that makes miniature models of factories.

volatile oil Scary-sounding manufactured product that was Virtucon's sole money-making endeavor before Dr. Evil launched himself into space in 1967, making room for Number 2 to run the company.

volcano, secret hollowed-out Locale the 1999 Dr. Evil had requested that his 1969 Number 2 find for a lair. It is located on a tropical island in the Caribbean. On the side of the volcano is a mammoth stone bust of Dr. Evil's face, à la Mt. Rushmore.

WELCOME TO MY HOLLOWED-OUT VOLCANO.

Volkswagen Beetle, convertible Austin's

time machine is a psychedically painted convertible
Volkswagen Beetle. When it is driven really fast – fast
enough to leave flaming tread marks – and when a
destination date is plugged into the dashboard
computer, the car will take off into the predetermined
past or future. *See* **product placement.**

Vulcan, the *See* **Project Vulcan.**

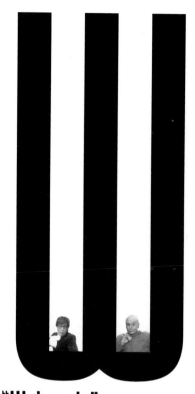

"Wait a tic" Austin's swinger parlance for "Hold up for a moment."

Wang Popular Chinese surname. When Dr. Evil's moon ship, which looks like a flying penis, passes over a Chinese Communist classroom, a teacher shouts, "Wang!" It seems at first that he is alerting the class to Dr. Evil's ship, but he is actually calling on one of his students to pay attention and stop looking out the window.

warm liquid goo phase see **Reanimation Process.**

warranty card for Swedish-made penis-enlarger pump, filled out by Austin Powers One of the items kept in storage for Austin while he is cryogenically frozen.

washroom attendant, blind
When Austin goes to the bathroom in a Las Vegas casino, looking for Number 2, he notices that the washroom attendant is a blind man. Seconds later, a gregarious Texan stranger bursts into the room, swinging the bathroom door into the face of the pathetic attendant.

water bottle
See **SCOTT EVIL button.**

water cooler
Device in offices throughout the world that not only dispenses fresh water, but also serves as an informal meeting place for co-workers. It is at the water cooler that Dr. Evil has his first awkward encounter with Frau Farbissina after they have had sex the night before.

weapons, nuclear
The president of the United States is upset that he cannot nuke Dr. Evil and instead has to pay him his blackmail money. "I got nukes up the yin-yang," he tells his advisors. "Just let me launch one, for Chrissakes."

webbed feet
Condition in which a human has abnormal skin growth between the toes, thus allowing for, say, easy paddling in water sports. Dr. Evil's mother, a fifteen-year-old French prostitute named Chloe, had webbed feet.

wedding presents
Basil's wedding gifts to Austin and Vanessa include a fruit basket and a spice rack. Even Dr. Evil gave Austin a wedding present. After Vanessa the Fembot's true identity is revealed, Dr. Evil's prerecorded

voice emits a message from her mouth that says, "Here's your wedding present, Mr. Powers, a kamikaze bride from me, Dr. Evil." Then she explodes. It is unlikely that Dr. Evil purchased his gift at a registry.

wedding tackle
One of the many nicknames Austin has conferred on his genitalia.

wee Extremely tiny. Mini-Me is "so wee" that he gives Fat Bastard "the willies."

Wheelbarrow, The See *Powers' Kama Sutra, Austin.*

woodpecker Bird native to North America, also known as a "pecker." When Dr. Evil's moon ship, which looks like a flying penis, passes over a couple walking in the woods, a man points to the sky and shouts, "Pecker!" It seems as if he is pointing to Dr. Evil's ship, but he actually thought he had seen a woodpecker.

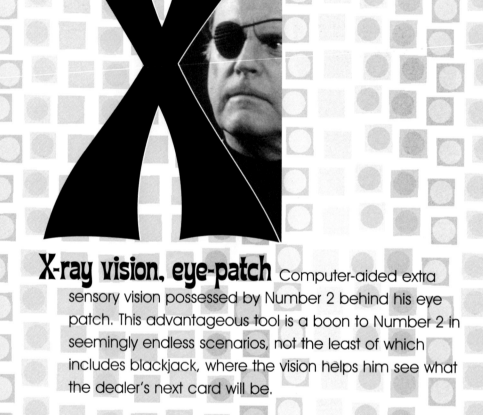

X-ray vision, eye-patch Computer-aided extra
sensory vision possessed by Number 2 behind his eye
patch. This advantageous tool is a boon to Number 2 in
seemingly endless scenarios, not the least of which
includes blackjack, where the vision helps him see what
the dealer's next card will be.

y

yin-yang Whereas in Chinese philosophy the yin and the yang intermingle beautifully to produce all that comes to be, a "yin-yang" is a much more base concept, essentially signifying an anus. When the president of the United States is frustrated that he cannot "nuke" Dr. Evil and instead has to pay him his blackmail money, the president loses his temper. "I got nukes up the yin-yang," he tells his advisors. "Just let me launch one, for Chrissakes."

Zappa, Moon Unit See **Elite Moon Unit.**

"Zip it" An order to be quiet. Dr. Evil tells his son, Scott, to zip it after his insolent offspring calls him "numb-nuts" and questions his math skills. See **Sshhh!; bag of sshhh!;** and **preemptive sshhh!**

Zoroastrianism Sixth-century Persian religion. When Dr. Evil was fourteen, a Zoroastrian named Vilma ritualistically shaved his testicles.